OUR ROAD
WITHOUT
BOUNDARIES

Revealing the Codes

Our Road without Boundaries.

For information contact:

Phone: +855 10 99 88 84

+354 821 1977

http://OurRoadwithoutBoundaries.com

http://AlexanderEvengroen.com

http://HuniHunfjord.com

Cover design, book design, editing and formatting by Alexander Evengroen & Huni Hunfjord.

ISBN: 978-9935-9342-8-4

First Edition: May, 2017.

Alexander Evengroen

YOUR MILLION DOLLAR SUCCES COACH

Húni Húnfjörð

TOP 1% MINDSET COACH

YOUR GROWTH IS MY FOCUS

About Alexander Evengroen

Alexander is a seasoned professional in Public Speaking, business development, Real Estate, Social Media, Sales & Marketing, plus a proven leader with the ability to leverage past experience and amazing creative knowledge towards the attainment of company goals.

He has a background in both start-up and working with fast growth innovative companies and specialize in building a company's capabilities to rapidly increase revenue, service levels and profits.

He has Great leadership, organizational and supervisory skills.

When speaking to corporate and business audiences, Alexander relates the ever-growing challenges of the 21st century workplace to his own, at times hilarious, at times deadly serious, trials and tribulations in the wild lands of the world.

Alexander is a global citizen; he has lived and worked all over Asia, Europe and Africa. He loves traveling and enjoying different cultures and people across the world.

Alexander's goal is to help you achieve your personal and business goals faster and easier than you ever imagined.

Alexander Evengroen has consulted for more than 200 companies and addressed more than 100.000 people in 1,000+ talks and seminars throughout Holland, Singapore, Cambodia, China, Ghana, South Africa and many other countries worldwide. As a Keynote speaker, motivational speaker and seminar leader, he addresses thousands of people each year.

He has studied, researched, written and spoken for many years in the fields of development, sales, management, business, philosophy and psychology.

He is the author and publisher of many books with his top rated best seller 'How to become a great Manager' that have been translated into different languages.

He speaks to corporate and public audiences on the subjects of Personal and Professional Development, including the executives and staff of many large corporations.

His exciting talks and seminars on Leadership, Selling, Self-Esteem, Goals, Strategy, Creativity and Success Psychology bring about immediate changes and long-term results.

He has traveled and worked in many countries on six continents, and speaks four languages.

Specialized in Public Speaking, Motivation, Training & Coaching and International Business Development.

Thanks to a handful of successful business results and being surrounded by amazing talent, I'm able to wake every day and focus on making the world a better place by serving others.

He's been referred to as an Entrepreneur, Solutions Strategist for Business, Public Speaker, Personal and Professional Coach, Author, Mentor, Philanthropist...you can use whatever label you wish.

His purpose in life is, "To Aid Others, Act on Ideas, and Achieve Sensational Results." Much of his time is spent as a trusted adviser to organizations and individuals around the world regarding professional and personal development.

He is an author, Serial entrepreneur, Success coach, and consultant who speaks regularly on a range of topics that include critical thinking, leadership, success, mindset, communication, sales, and finding your purpose.

The importance of teamwork and leadership skills were drilled into him early in life, while working on my first direct sales job. He transferred to the business world and held several executive and management positions, before stepping out to build his own start up online clothing company. Along the way he has tackled several other challenges not listed here. Alexander is currently still partners in, or owner of, several other companies in a variety of industries.

Many people connect with him to take a look at their business or personal life with a different set of glasses. His intention is to find the uncommon where others see the common, by filtering in versus filtering out. He is here to serve, and if he can't help, he'll point you in the direction of someone who can!

He advocates that with the right attitudes, and especially by treating our toughest problems as challenges and adventures, we can achieve more than we ever thought possible. Alexander's presentations are ideal for, corporate events, conferences and staff training days where, alongside technical topics geared for the business, there is also a need for a captivating motivational message.

"Your Million Dollar Success Coach"

- Alexander Evengroen

About Huni Hunfjord

Huni Hunfjord is the co-founder of Focus Gym ♥♥ Be you!, creator of the Watchon Indicator brand, senior managing director at IcyDesign ehf. Huni is the author of "Top 1% Parents Raise Top 1% Children", "Sleeping Habits and Routines" and "The Mentorian" also known as "Læringinn". He is a coach and serial entrepreneur.

Huni has always been fascinated by the human mind and human behaviors. He first started in the computer industry only 8 years old and created his first computer game in the old DOS PC operating system. Computers are easy because they do just what they are told, no less and not more, but his fascination with the unpredictability of the human mind captured his imagination early on.

After a few human errors and conflicts during his university studies in computer science, he was forced to pick a new major, he choose business administration and management. His obsession with human behavior lead him to pick that major believe it or not.

It took the inexperienced Icelandic foreigner then living in USA about two semesters to master how to interact with the teachers and get good grades without studying at all.

The reason he searched for an easy way out, was because he thought that he was dyslexic at the time, because he fell asleep each time he tried to read a school book, or any book for that matter. Therefore he felt forced to find ways to create success without reading.

By old fashioned human interaction with the teachers and by listening in the classroom he was able to pull his grade from a 1.8 GPA to a 3.1 GPA with ease, staying on the dean's list the rest of his way through the university.

It was not until he turned 34 years old, having only read one entire book up until then, when he realized that all his attempts at reading had failed because he was not interested in the topic, they simply did not capture his focus.

The simple truth will set so many of us free. Since then he has read over 30 books each year and is steadily increasing the amount of books he reads each year.

He has spent the last few years learning from the best coaches in the world in mindset, marketing and wealth.

One of Huni's most educational journeys of growth, was during his time when he was working in a multi-level-marketing company. He learned some hard and valuable lessons there, everything from being annihilated to being embraced and loved. How to deal with rejection and how to turn a no into a yes.

Huni's passion is helping people grow spiritually, mentally and economically. Huni's greatest joy is to feel the appreciation of making a difference, true difference, in another peoples lives.

His growth and social media exposure has explode since 2015. He has been referred to as a life changer, a life saver, a serial entrepreneur, a philanthropist, a motivational public figure, a coachable student and a great coach, any of those he is proud to be called.

When Huni starts a new venture, he is often faced with the dilemma like so many entrepreneurs are, he gets impatient and wants more and faster results, which is what makes him a great entrepreneur, he is always seeking ways to increase his productivity and performance, measuring it over and over again, knowing the perfection does not exist but growth does. Done is the new perfect.

He knows that as long as you are growing it's worth it.

He is willing to go the extra mile every single time.

"Your Growth is My Focus"

- Huni Hunfjord

Table of Contents

1. Building Quality into Your Team

Building a Quality Team

Quality is often viewed in terms of corporate culture, multiple departmental task forces and the solution for the entire company. In this chapter, we will instead, view these ideas as they might be applied by team leaders with a small permanent staff under their control.

Quality has become the philosophers' stone of management practice with consultants and gurus trying to charm normal companies into medal winning champions.

We hear more and more stories about companies with more workers and mounting debts being transformed into happy teams and healthy profits; never a day goes by without a significant improvement, a money saving suggestion or a gigantic leap in efficiency. With this belief of success from these quality programs, there has evolved a proscriptive mythology of correct practice which has several draw backs:

- The edicts call for nothing less than a companywide, senior-management led program.

- The commitment to a single formula has a limited effect, it excludes innovation outside these boundaries, and reduces the differentiation which such programs profess to engender the emphasis on a single task, specially formed group's shifts the focus away from the ordinary daily tasks.

Of course, these criticisms do not invalidate the ideas of quality but are simply to suggest that the principles might well be viewed from another angle and applied at a different level.

We attempts to provide a new perspective by re-examining some of the basic beliefs of quality in the context to a small, established team could be simply to ask what a great team leader would do with their staff.

TEAM work

Together

Everybody

Achieves

More

What is Quality?

In current management writings, quality has come to refer to a whole class of practices which themselves which have resulted in beneficial side-effects; as a manager, you will want to take advantage of these benefits as well.

The Customer

In simple terms, to optain quality has something to do with satisfying the expectations of the customers. Concern for the wishes and needs of customers becoming the focus for every decision you make. What the customer wants and needs will become what the company will provide. This is not philanthropy, this is basic survival.

Through careful education by competitors, the customer has begun to exercise their spending power in favor of quality goods and services. While quality is not the sole criteria when selecting a particular supplier, it has become an important differentiator to accomondate the needs and will of the customers.

The World Evolves Around Your Customer and Client, not around You!!

If a ten cent ball-point runs dry in one month and another ten cent ball-point lasts for three months then the second ball-point is the one which the customer will buy again and which they recommends to others - even if it costs a little more.

The makers of the first ball-point may have higher profit margins, but eventually no customers will buy the ball-point anymore. Without quality in the product, a company sacrifices customers, good revenue and ultimately its own existence. In practical terms, quality is that something extra which will be perceived by the customer as a good reason for either paying more or for buying a product or service again and again.

In the case where the product is a service, quality is measured by how well the job is done and especially with whether the customer is happy about the whole operation or not.

In this respect quality in many cases does cost more but the loss is regained in the price customers are prepared to pay and in the increase of business.

Reliability

The clearest evedence of quality is in the reliability of a product. How the product works. To prevent problems from arising after the product is shipped, the quality must be checked beforehand and the best time to check quality is throughout the whole design and manufacturing process.

The old method of quality control was to test the completed products and then to rework the whole process to remove any problems or defects. Thus while the original production time was short, the time it took to rework the whole process was long.

The new approach to quality simply asserts that if testing becomes an integral part of each stage of production, the production time may increase but the rework time will disappear all together. Further, you will catch and solve most problems which the final quality-check would miss but which the customer will find on the first day of using the product.

To achieve this requires an environment where the identification of errors is considered to be not a bad thing. It an environment where the only bad bugs are the ones which got away.

One of the most hallowed doctrines of quality is that of 0 defects. It is a glorious objective to have "0 defects" as a focus, it is the assertion that nothing less will suffice and that no matter how high the quality of any product, it can still be improved.

It is a paradox in that it is an aim which is contrary to reason, and like the paradoxes of many other religions it holds an inner truth. This is why the advocates of quality often seem a little crazy at times.

People Are the Most Valuable Resource

While quality has its own reward in terms of increased long-term sales, the methods used to achieve this quality also have other benefits. In seeking to improve the quality of a product, manufacturers have found that the people best placed to make substantial contributions are the workforce. Your people are your most valuable resource when it comes to quality.

It is this change in perspective from the management to the workforce which is the most significant value in your search for quality.

From this change in perspective we now have new managerial viewpoints aimed at the empowerment of the workforce. Decision-making is now in your front line, active staff involvement in the company's advancements and from this new perspective, new organizational structures have evolved, exemplified in "Quality Loop".

Without getting off the topic too much, it is important to examine the benefits of this approach. For such delegation to be safely and effectively undertaken, the management has to train the workforce, not necessarily directly, and not all at once, but often within the quality loop themselves using a single "architect" or a simple confidential coaching.

The workforce had to learn how to hold meetings, how to analyze problems, how to make decisions, how to present solutions, how to implement and how to evaluate the change.

These traditionally high level managerial privileges are devolved to the whole staff.

Not only does this develop great talent but it also stimulates overall interest. Staff begins to look not only for problems but also for the solutions. You create a culture of intrapreneurs, people who start to think of the company as their own, so to speak.

Simple ideas become simply implemented. The accountant finally gets the filing cabinet moved closer to the office, the sales teams follow an agenda, and the software division creates a new bulletin board for the golf club. The environment is created where people see problems and fix them.

Bigger problems have more complex solutions. One outcome of the search for quality in Asia is the system of Just-In-Time flow control. In this system, goods arrive at each stage of the manufacturing process just before they are needed and are not made until they are needed for the next stage.

This diminishes storage requirements and inventory costs of stock. Another outcome has been the increased flexibility of the production line.

Time to change from one product run to the next product was identified as a huge obstacle in providing the customer with the desired range of products and quantities, and so the whole workforce became engaged in changing the existent practices and even in redesigning the machinery needed for these processes.

The Long Term

We believe that the most significant shift in perspective which comes with the introduction of good quality is that long term success is given precedence over short term advances. The repeated sale and recommendation are more important than one month's sales figures. We have a need to keep moving forward in a stressful situation regarding overbooking an agenda or schedule. With the product reliability is referred to as quality is before sales. We can not sell if the product or service is not up to the highest standards.

Time is invested today into saving more time in the future and in making products which work first and every time.

Your Team Quality

While the rescue of an entire corporation may rest primarily with higher management, the fate of a team rests with the team manager. The team manager has the authority to define the micro-culture of the work force.

It is by the deliberate application of the principles of quality that the team manager can gain for the team the same benefits which quality can provide for a corporation.

The best ideas for any team are likely to come from them as the aim of the team manager must be to act as a promoter through prompts and by example.

Getting Started

There will be no overnight success in what we do. To be lasting, quality must become a daily habit and a habit is accustomed practice. This takes a lot of time and training, although not necessarily formal training but possibly the sort of reinforcement you might give to any aspect of creating good practice. To adjust your staff to higher quality, you must first make it an important issue. Here is what you can do:

The first idea is to become excited about one thing at a time and initially look for a quick fix. Find a problem and start to talk about it with the whole team. Do not delegate it to an individual but make it an issue for the whole team to deal with.

Choose a related problem like "how to get the correct information in time" and take everybody's opinions and suggestions and valuate them and get the problem solved as a team. Demand speed against a clear target.

There is no need to allocate large amounts of resource or time to this, simply bring up the problem and make a fuss. When a good solution comes, praise it by rewarding the whole team and ensure that the aspects of increased effectiveness are highlighted since this will create the criteria for success. Now find the next problem and repeat the process.

The next idea is the regular weekly meeting to discuss the quality. Of course meetings can be complete time wasters, so this strategy requires good care.

The good thing is that regularity will lead to good habits. The formality will provide a simple opportunity for the expression of ideas and the inclusion of the whole team at the meeting will underline the collective responsibility. By using the regular meeting, you can establish the ground rules of accepted behavior and at the same time train the team in effective desired techniques.

One problem is that the focus on any one particular issue may quickly loose its value. A solution is to have frequent focus shifts so that you and your team maintain the freshness and enthusiasm.

Other benefits are that continual shifts in emphasis will train your team to be more flexible, and provide the opportunity for them to raise any issues. The sooner the team takes over the definition of the "Let's come up with the next solution" the better.

Initial Phases

All initial phases are delicate. The team will be feeling greater responsibility without the extra confidence. Thus you must concentrate on supporting and improving their development. In essence you will train them in their management skills.

You could get outside help with this but by undertaking the challenge yourself, you keep control. You are shaping the team so that they will reflect your own approach and use your own criteria. Later they will develop their own criteria and skills, but even then they will understand your thinking and so your decisions. You are creating mini-you versions.

One trap to avoid is that the team may focus on the wrong category of problems. You must make it very clear that any problem which they tackle should be:

- related to their own job or environment

- something they can change

This prevents gripe sessions about wages and holidays.

As with all team work, the main problem is transparency. You should provide the team with a notice board and charts specifically for any quality related problems. These can then be left on display as a permanent record of what was agreed upon.

If you can, steer your team to some problems with a simple solution and with obvious measurable benefits. A quick, sharp success story will motivate your team to carry on.

Team Building

To thrive, a quality push must involve the enthusiasm of the entire team. As team leader, you must create the right energy boost for this to happen. Many aspects of team building can be addressed while high quality remains the main focus.

You must create the environment where each team member feels totally happy to express an idea or a problem and this can only be done if there is no fear of being incorrect. No idea is wrong, merely none optimal.

In each suggestion there is at least a small diamond to be found and someone should notice it and if possible, build upon it. Any behavior which seeks laughter at the expense of others must be eliminated.

One very effective method is to write down the ground rules and to display them as a constant reminder for everyone, something like:

- all criticism must be friendly and constructive

- all problems are our problems

- BUGS WANTED: DEAD OR ALIVE (but not for long)

- if it saves time later, do it now

Another great method is to constantly talk about the team as the plural pronoun: "we decided", "we will do this", "and we'll get back to you".

This is extremely effective if it is used in conversation with outsiders (especially management) close to the team. Praise and reward the entire team. Get the team wider fame by a success story in an internal magazine or internal website.

It is extremely importantly that you enable failure. If the team is unable to try out ideas without room for any errors, then the room of their solutions will be severely limited.

Instead, a failure should be an opportunity to gain knowledge what is power and to praise any safe-guards which were included in the plan.

Shared Coaching

An important part of team communication is the idea of mutual support. If you can introduce the idea that all problems are owned by the entire team then each person will be able to seek help and support when needed from every other team member.

One way to support this idea is to encourage shared coaching. If one team member knows techniques or has information which would be useful to the rest, then encourage them to share it. This will definitely raise the profile, confidence and self-esteem of the trainer at the same time as benefiting the entire group and if there is one person who might never have anything useful to communicate then send this person to a conference or training session to find something.

Statistics

One of the main beliefs of quality programs is the idea of monitoring the problem being addressed.

Statistical quality control. Very simply, if you can't measure an improvement, the problem probably isn't there to start with. Gathering statistics has several benefits in applying quality:

- it identifies the problem
- it allows improvement to be monitored
- it provides an objective standard for the rejection of an idea
- it can validate perceived expense in terms of observed improvements or changes
- it will motivate staff by providing a display of accomplishments

One of the funny positive side effects are, that some problems simply disappear when you try to watch them closely.

Good statistics must be collected in an objective manner, the outcome should be a simple graphical chart that is frequently updated to designate progress, and these results must be displayed where the whole team can see them. If your team provides product support, then you might monitor the number of recurrence enquiries or the average response time of your team.

In the long term, it may be right to implement automatic gathering of needed statistics on a wide range of issues such as complaints, bug reports, contact requests, delivery, and so on.

Ultimately these may either provide early warning of unforeseen problems, or relative data for new quality improvement projects. It is vital that they focus upon a problem and not upon an individual's performance or else all the positive motivation of team involvement will be lost.

Projects

Clarity of WHY, this is the key to success. You need a simple, stated objective which everybody understands and which everybody can see achieved.

Any plan to improve the quality or success of the team must contain:

- the objective
- The WHY
- the method
- the statistcs for monitoring the outcome
- the agreed criteria for completion or restriction

By sticking to this format, you provide the owners of each of the plans with a simple mechanism for peer recognition and yet enable them to manage their own failure with elegance.

For a small established team, the customer includes any other part of the company with which the team work together. Thus any themes regarding customer satisfaction can be developed with respect to these so called center customers.

In the end, the effectiveness of your team will be judged by the reports of how well they provide products or services for others.

A simple improvement might be for a team member to really talk to someone from each of these center customer groups and to ask about any problems and get feedback.

This is usually the best place to look for problems that are easy to solve.

The direct benefit may be to your customer, but in the long run better communications will lead to fewer misunderstandings and therfore less rework.

Building Quality

Great Quality costs less than its lack. Look after the money and the profits will take care of themselves. To build a great quality product, you must do two things:

- create the design and the procedures

- take in features to aid quality checking

It is a question of attitude. If one of the team spots a modification in the design or the procedures which will have a long term benefit, then that must be given priority over the immediate schedule.

The design is never perfect. You should allocate time specifically to discussing improvement.

In this process you should not aim at actual improvements in the sense of added features or faster performance, but towards making it more simple. This is an adjunct to the normal design or production operations. The extra mile which lesser teams would not go for sure.

Many products and services do not lend themselves to quality 24-hour care.

These should be improved so that the quality becomes easily tracked. This may be a simple invitation for the customer to comment, or it could be a full design modification to provide an easy testing routine.

Any product whose quality cannot be tracked should naturally become a source of deep concern to the whole team, until you create the mechanism to do so.

One of the not often used sources of quality in design and production in the developing world is documentation. This is frequently seen as the final problem at product release, sometimes even delegated to another group, yet the writing of such documentation can be used as an important tool for the explanation of ideas.

Documenting also protects the group from the loss of any single individual. You don't lose the knowledge, but instead protect the process, so someone else can step in, in case of a person leaving the team.

In devising a mechanism for monitoring quality, many teams will produce test procedures.

As problem emerge, new procedures should be added which specifically identify this problem and so check for the solution. Even after the problem is solved the new procedures should be monitored and see if the changed procedure may catch another problem.

The test set should develop to cover all known possibilities of fault and its application should, where possible, be automated and updated.

Role Changes

As your team develops your role as leader it changes slightly. You become a cross between a Pope and a American football captain, providing the vision and the values while shouting like crazy from the center of the field. Although you retain the final say, the team begins to make decisions in the process.

The toughest part, as with all delegation, is in accepting the team decision even though you may not always agree. You must never countermand a small decision.

If you have to overrule the team, it is important that you explain your reasons clearly so that they understand the criteria and this will both justify your intervention and coach the team in good decision-making practices.

Another role which you assume is that of both shield and boundary between the team and the rest of the company. A shield in that you protect the team from the vagaries of less enlightened managers, a boundary in that you keep the team informed about factors relevant to their decisions.

Eventually, the team will be delegating to you tasks, which only you as manager, can perform on its behalf.

Quality for Profit

By applying the Quality principles to an established team, the team leader can enjoy the benefits so actively sought after by large corporations.

The KEY to all this is the attitude and the insistence on the priority of quality. As a team leader, you have the power to define the ethics of your staff by using quality as the focus, you also can accrue its riches.

2. Where Are You and What You Want

Where Are You and What Do You Want

Knowing your number. Why is it so important to know your numbers?

What does it trigger in our minds when we write down what we consume or what we spend our money on?

Do you know where you stand today? If not, I assure you that you need to know it to be able to reach your goals, to be able to measure where you stand, how far you have come and much is left of the journey. It is like planning a trip to a certain city on a map, if you don't know where your starting point is, it will be hard to plan the trip and it will be almost impossible to calculate how long the trip will take.

Most people cannot tell you how much they spend on food each month, or how many calories they burn, how many calories they eat, how much quality time they spend with their children or how much money they need to be financially free so they can spend more time with their children, travel more and work less.

To measure something and then measure it again, makes it possible for us to tell if we are going in the right direction, doing it right or not, whether a person is steadily growing or slowly dying. Whatever the goal you have in mind for yourself as a parent or as an entrepreneur, it will be very hard to know when you have reached it, if you don't know where you stand today and where you want to be standing tomorrow or at at predefined date in the future.

Now let's talk a little about the exceptions to the rule, sometimes goals can be measured without knowing where you are at today, these goals are the exception to the rule but yet we still need to know our numbers during our journey there, to know when we have arrived. For example, if your goal would be to make $10,000 per month, you need to know what you make each month, from when you start your journey and each week during your journey there.

When you reach your goal of $10,000 per month, you might find out that this goal did not solve what you thought it would solve. It might not be enough to make you financially free like you thought in the beginning of the journey.

For you to be able to set a realistic goal, to know when you reach it, knowing that this goal will solve your problem, you first need to know what you lack right now to be able to succeed.

That is why I consider setting your goals, knowing your numbers, knowing where you stand now and where you need to stand to reach your goals, to be a better way of actually reaching your goals then to just wing it and go for it. When you finally reach your goals, you always need to have a new goal ready, the next goal! The next step in the ladder.

That will help you sustain your goal and to grow even further and it is very important when handling your fears, which we will discuss later on, in this book. I like to call him BOB, but let's not get ahead of ourselves.

It is totally up to you if you want to set a goal now and find out when you reach the goal if it was great enough for you or not, but I will always recommend that you know where you stand now and based on that information you make a decision on how much or what you need, to be able to solve the problem. This applies to almost all the goals we set in life, not just financial goals.

When we start to monitor the things we do today, we write them down, but why do we need to write them down?

The secret about writing down what you do, is so much more than just knowing what you do and where you stand, let me explain. Let me tell you what writing these things down, does for a human being.

I am going to use two examples to illustrate this point.

1. Writing down what and how much you consume.

2. Keeping a simple spending diary by writing down what you purchase, labeling it whether it is a necessary or unnecessary purchase.

Food Diary

Let's start with the food diary. When we start to write down all the things that we consume, we are doing so much more than just writing it down. We can go to several free websites and get the nutritional values from our consumption and get the facts about how many vitamins we are consuming and how much more or less we need to be taking.

How much of the essential minerals, vitamins, sugars and fats we really need, that is in our current diet. We also get a list of all the crap that we are consuming, the surplus sugar amount and the types of fats we consume (including partial hydrogenation fats).

Hydrogenated fats are unnatural fats that are terrible for your health. I am just squeezing this message in here because I can and because your health is a big part of your success story. If you succeed and once you reach that destination and don't have you health by then, then why bother?

There are three general types of fats in foods are; Saturated (e.g., butter, lard) -

Monounsaturated (e.g., olive or canola oils) and Polyunsaturated (e.g., omega-6 oils like sunflower or safflower oil, or omega-3 oils like fish and flaxseed oils). Hydrogenation (or, more accurately, partial hydrogenation, as the process is incomplete) is the forced chemical addition of hydrogen into omega-6 polyunsaturated oils to make them hard at room temperatures, primarily used as a cheaper and less perishable substitute for butter and you should avoid it if at all possible. There, now I have informed you a bit about the fat's you should avoid if possible.

This part of the food diary is the obvious part of keeping a food diary. We get the facts, but what else happens in our brain when we keep a diary like that? We start to be aware of what we are actually consuming and therefore immediately start to make better decisions when we are deciding what we consume.

Some might make better decisions because they don't want a negative score in their diary, some might do it because they don't want to have a written proof anywhere of how unhealthy their diet actually is, some might do it because they just really want to eat healthy and some might have some other reason for changing his or her consumption patterns that is triggered by writing everything down in the food diary. The bottom line is, the reason does not matter, what matters is that you have already begun to change your life the minute you decided to start writing down what you consume! Your focus has shifted. You become aware and now you can see.

Spending Diary

The type of spending diary I recommend is to keep it as simple as possible. I recommend not listing every single object, at least not to start with. I know some of the dominant left brained people would like to list everything down, but that is overkill and not the point. The most important part of the spending diary is to write down whether your purchase was necessary or unnecessary. Example:

Date	What	Amount	Un/Necessary
01/04	Groceries	$212	N
02/04	Beer at the pub	$15	U
05/04	Parking - New York	$20	N
07/04	Doctor - St Mary's	$80	N
09/04	Donuts	$12	U
09/04	Movies	$28	U
09/04	White wine & Pizza	$74	U

The main reason why I suggest doing this as simple as possible is so that you will continue doing this and start making changes in your spending habits right away.

Over 90% of people, who go into all the details right away, quit during their first month of keeping a spending diary. Be careful, start slowly, this is a marathon not a sprint.

What is the best way to eat a whole elephant? One bite at a time!

This kind of diary does similar things for you, as the food diary. You will be able to see what you are actually spending your money on, how much you spend on groceries and so forth. You are forced each time to think about, whether this is something that is necessary or unnecessary and you will start making better decisions right away, even before spending anything.

Let's say you are improving your life on many levels right now and you decide you only need to start putting aside extra $50 dollars on top of what you're already putting aside each month, but you have no idea where to find that money.

I assure you after monitoring your spending, you will find the $50 extra you need in your spending diary.

By making a decision to start writing down everything you spend your money on and labeling it whether it is necessary or unnecessary, you have already started the transformation.

By starting a spending diary you have already shifted your mindset and focus towards finding the unnecessary spending habits and changing them.

Start each month by calculating, on another piece of paper, all the things you spent money on last month and then sum together all the things you considered to be necessary versus all the things you considered unnecessary.

This can be implemented and applied to anything you want to achieve. You can write down each day, how you feel and set a goal of how you want to feel. Happiness is just a choice, you can choose to be happy and you can choose to start right now.

By monitoring whether you are happy or not, will help you in triggering a state of happiness, once you realize that today your are not, but remember that once you get in the habit of writing it down, most likely you will slowly stop having bad days, because your focus is on being happy.

You can write down how much quality time you spend with your children and how much time you would like to spend with your children. Only your imagination limits what you can monitor and what goals you set for your life.

Summary

- Writing down what you spend your money on, helps you shift your spending habits and you can move towards your financial goals.

- Writing down what you consume will shift you're eating habits towards your health goals.

- Writing down what you do and how you do it, gives you a clear picture of where you are today and makes it easier for you to monitor your progress while reaching your goals.

- Write down your feelings and maintain it, like happiness for example. Set goals for how you want to feel as well as for what you want to achieve.

3. Achieve Your Goals

How to Achieve Your Goals

I have made steady progress on my goals every day without incredible doses of willpower or mega doses of motivation.

I will share how I use this strategy and how you can apply it to your own life to improve your health, wealth and your work.

The Problem with Setting Goals

If you're anything like the typical human, then you have dreams and goals in your life. In fact, there are probably many things that you would like to accomplish.

That's fantastic, but there is one common big mistake we often make when it comes to setting goals (I made this mistake as well).

The problem is that we set a deadline, but not a schedule.

We focus on the end results that we want to achieve and the deadline we want to do it by. We say things like, "I want to lose 10 kilos by the spring" or "I want to add 5 kilometer to my running distance in the next 12 weeks."

The concern with this is that if we don't mysteriously hit the subjective timeline that we set in the beginning, then we feel like a failure, even if we are much better than we were at the start. The end result, sadly, is that we often give up if we don't reach our goal by the original deadline.

As I've mentioned this idea before. For example, in making the mistake of putting your goals before your identity or in choosing life changing transformations over daily lifestyle choices.

Here's the good news. There's a great way and it's simple.

The Power of Setting Great Schedules

A better way to approach your goals is to set a schedule to operate by rather than a crazy deadline to perform by.

Instead of giving yourself an unrealistic deadline to accomplish a specific goal you should choose a goal that is most important to you and then set a schedule to work towards it consistently.

That might not sound like a big change, but it is compounding though time, small steps each day.

How to Achieve Your Goals

Most of the time, I try to implement my ideas myself and not just someone who shares their opinion, so allow me to explain this strategy by using two real examples from my own life.

Writing a book

I try to publish a new book every 2 years, I've never missed a scheduled date. Sometimes the book is shorter than expected, sometimes it's not as compelling as I had hoped, and sometimes it's not as useful as it could be but it gets out to the world and into people's hands and with the great feedback I've gotten for each one, the books are getting better and better.

The results of this simple schedule have been amazing. Our little community has grown, seemingly without effort. We now have over 23,000 people who bought my books. Onwards to 25,000 with this copy you just bought, thank you!

Imagine if I had set a crazy deadline for myself instead, like writing 5 books per year. There's no way I would have written that fast and with good stories and content, and if I didn't reach my goal, then I would have felt like a failure and be even more demotivated for my next thing.

Instead, we are slowly building great content and great quality books that help people move forward and learn a lesson that makes a difference for them.

Exercise

Back in August, I decided that I wanted to do 100 pushups in a row. When I tried it the first time, I only got 54.

In the past, I might have set a deadline for myself: "Do 100 pushups by December 31st."

Instead, I decided to set a schedule for my workouts. I started doing pushup workouts every Monday, Wednesday, and Friday. So far, the only workouts I've missed is when I was sick.

I have no total pushup goal for any single workout. The goal is simply to do the workout. Just like I have no goal for any single article that I write. The goal is to publish the article.

The result, of course, is that after doing 87 pushup workouts I've made a lot of progress. If you push yourself by committing to what you really want the results will follow.

Focus on the Practice.

In both writing and exercise, I made consistent progress towards my goals not by setting a deadline for my performance, but by sticking to a fantastic schedule.

Productive and successful people practice the things that are important to them on a consistent basis. The best weightlifters are in the gym at the same time every week. The best writers are sitting down at the keyboard every day. And this same principle applies to the best leaders, parents, managers, musicians, and doctors.

The strange thing is that for top performers, it's not about the performance itself but it's about the continual practice.

The focus is on doing the action, not on achieving any goal by a certain time.

The schedule is your friend.

You can't predict when you'll have a stroke of genius, an amazing bestselling story, paint a beautiful portrait, or shoot an incredible picture, but the correct schedule can make sure that you're working when that stroke of genius happens.

You can't predict when your mind and body feels like setting a new record, but the schedule can make sure that you're in the gym whether you feel like it or not.

It's about practicing the skill, not performing at a certain level. We're talking about practice. Not a game.

If you want to be the type of person who achieves things on a constant basis, then give yourself a good schedule to follow, not a deadline to race towards.

Achieve Your Goals

To really achieve your goals, first you'll have to determine exactly what they are. Don't let this process overwhelm you. Rely on your gut feeling.

Set a 5 minute timer and get all of your goals down on paper without thinking about how difficult it will be to achieve them.

After this, go back and think what changes you'll have to implement or routine adjustments you'll have to make in order to make your goals become reality. Whatever you do, don't put your list in a dusty shoebox somewhere, but instead have it somewhere were its easy to refer to it regularly.

Next thing is to keep things clean around you. Clutter doesn't just actually get in the way, it's technically proven to distract you. Think of it not only as a physical mess, but a mental one. Extra objects on your desk attract your attention, and your brain must constantly resolve the presence of these items with the ones that are actually relevant to your work.

Speaking of presence, consider that some of the stuff that's been there awhile is likely dragging you out of the moment. As for any items you might feel symbolically attached to, ask yourself a simple question: Is this thing inspiring me to achieve my goals, or does it serve another purpose?

Get rid of any distractions.

Your office desk might look like a photography lover's pristine dream, but if you fail to get rid of other distractions, your workspace will do you little good. Find ways to shut out family members break during work, social media notifications and private phone calls and appointments. Set a professional schedule for yourself and follow it, even if no one is there to check you. If you're doing professional work, look the part.

Become an early bird.

Sometimes, no matter how much you try to isolate yourself from daytime distractions such as kids, errands or even breaking news, it's hard to keep fully focused. One solution that's helped several successful entrepreneurs find time to work toward their goals is waking up very early. Sure, our bodies become programmed to waking up at the same time every day, and it will be difficult to adjust in the beginning. Don't expect to add three extra hours to your morning in the matter of a day. It takes time, patience and peace of mind to become an early bird. I changed this habit as well after my good friend Huni showed me what he did more by just waking up early.

Enjoy your weekends.

It's important to rest and recharge during the weekend, but it's also a smart idea to prepare yourself for the week ahead, including how you plan on achieving your goal.

When you wake up on Monday morning, don't let the alarm clock overwhelm you with the dread of routine dull chores. On Sunday night, set aside some time to select your outfit for the following days, plan meals and organize your weekly to-do list. You'll rest better, minimize any stress and have more time for the work you're loving. If you want to add a something extra to you morning routine, then add a motivational speech from yourself. Record your own voice motivating you to wake up early, find a powerful enough story to wake you up, your WHY, would be an example that would do the trick, as I know my friend Huni wakes up to his own voice each morning.

No more procrastinating.

You might start a given task only to find yourself wandering over to the freezer, checking email or Googling the names of the 45 Presidents of the United States of America. While procrastination may seem inevitable, try my 30-minute rule. Set a timer for 30 minutes, and commit to working on something you've been putting off for a long time. Who knows? You might gain some momentum and not feel like quitting once the time is up.

Find people who can help you.

No matter how driven you are, you'd be crazy to think you can achieve great success single-handedly. Even if someone else isn't aiding you directly, it is helpful to find a few individuals whom you can compete with, who will inspire you to persevere or hold you accountable for your actions and results.

A mentor can provide valuable advice so that you won't have to learn the basic lessons the hard way. You might benefit from somebody to keep you motivated and hold you accountable. Find specific people who can help you bridge the gap between where you are and where you want to go.

Play the role.

Think about who you want to be. How will that new and better version of yourself act? How will you think, act, speak and live? Chances are, you'll want to describe yourself as a humble yet very confident person. Sit up straight rather than slouch over. Look others straight in the eye and listen to what they say rather than gaze into the distance or let your mind wander off.

Be thoughtful about the words you use. If you can learn from others, make a good impression and discipline yourself to show the world your true aspirations, success will definitely follow.

Check your progress

You cannot just integrate new habits and ditch old ones. You have to make time to consistently evaluate yourself and others to make sure that you're on the right track. You might do this once you've achieved some lesser goals that will build toward a larger one, or if you've given yourself a deadline schedule regular review sessions.

During these checks with yourself, reflect on what you've been doing and determine whether it's working or how you might alter your plan. Let what you've accomplished inspire you to keep going and move forward.

Rewards yourself as a Motivation Tool.

If you plan to rewards yourself once you've achieved mini milestones, you'll have an additional incentive to continue and stay focused aside from the big goal in and of itself.

A milestone might take the form of reaching a certain number of followers on a social media account, getting up at 5 a.m. every day for the first week or saving an additional $1,000, $5,000 or $10,000. You might treat yourself to your favorite cake, a spa treatment, new recreational gear or just a lazy day off. Whatever the case, make sure your reward system is enticing enough to motivate you to work hard, but modest enough to be sustainable in the long run.

To-Do List.

Accepting criticism.

Remember we have positive and negative critique. Learn from critique to improve rather than taking negative feedback to heart or letting it get you down. Any feedback is doing something for you. Listen and learn, even when it is hard.

Following your passion.

Dreams are always a great drive to put effort in to your passion. If you truly love what you're doing, it's easier to achieve those goals, as opposed to being driven by financial motive.

Keep Learning.

Someone who's constantly learning and staying updated on any changes is in a better position to capitalize on his or her success.

Setting deadlines.

Put a planned finish date on paper to achieve a goal helps keep you on track to meet it. Once you've met it, create your next goal and set another hard for that one. Make sure you keep repeating it. Habit is the power.

Reach Goals together.

If you find a friend or college to reach your mutual goals, you will increase your success results by 1000% and learn how to achieve your goals.

This is so powerful.

If you have an accountability partner, which we call "a mutual goal getter", your progress will skyrocket for sure.

Your partner will hold you accountable for your improvement.

No more stalling in front of the TV when you stated that you will go three or four times per week to the gym.

Would you like to break your own agreement and look like a person who cannot be counted on in front of somebody whose opinion really matters to you? NO!

When things get hard, when the daily insanity starts to take over, when an event happens and you just stop progress with your goals.

Then your goal partner comes and saves the day.

But even with a mutual goal getter, you absolutely need to review your results once per week.

Let's combine two powerful concepts with a third one.

You have the goal partner and you want to have one actionable task each week.

So, why not do a weekly review call with them?

You call your partner every week at a fixed time....I call every Sunday at 6 p.m.

During the call you take turns and everybody tells the other one what was completed during the week and what the next actions for the coming week are.

Clear Goals

Most people would agree that the people who have clear goals are more successful than those who do not have any goals.

Let's take a look at leadership and management. Leadership is about doing the right things while management is about doing things right. Often when we study time management, we learn efficiency and make the assumption that we have the success formula solved.

The number one in any time management system should be to work on goals and as such, I use the following a one hour Goal Setting Exercise.

Spend 10 to 15 minutes writing down everything that is of any value too you. After the time is up, stop doing this and move to the next point.

The next step is to put down your lifetime goals. This is where you can dream. This might include traveling to Europe or Iceland, getting a university degree, living in a beautiful own build house at the ocean, etc. There are no rules to this brainstorming, simply make a list.

I have done this goal exercise many times and I tend to use the same list of lifetime goals and add to the list each time I do the exercise. Always trying to add a new one.

Next step is to list everything that you would do if you had only short time left to live. Part of the purpose of this exercise that I found works well for me is that it brings the truly important things into focus. Often I find things that I would do if I had a short time to live that are not listed on my life time goals.

Next is to put down your goals for this year. After doing the first three steps, you will find this step much easier than the others. These are the goals to focus on NOW.

This exercise will take less than an hour to complete. An hour spent clarifying your goals can save you hundreds of hours down the road.

4. Manifesting Your Desires

Manifesting Your Desires

We hear so many people talk about the law of attraction and yet so few really know what it is and how it really works. In short, you can get whatever you want in life as long as you know how this law works and how to use it.

Your mind is so powerful there is no way to explain what you truly can do when you set your mind to it. What is the law of attraction anyway, it describes the law of attracting something or repelling it. What do you need to do in order to attract the things you want and stop repelling them?

Let me start by telling you two stories from my life that explain how the law of attraction works.

Story One

When I was around 15 years old, I had just started playing basketball, but as tall as I was, around 191 cm (approx. 6´3) I was struggling to dunk the basketball. I had a talk with my father and told him I really wanted to be able to dunk the basketball, at the time I could only do that with a smaller ball, like a tennis ball.

My father did not know anything about basketball, but asked me if I could close my eyes and see myself dunking. I said yes. Then he asked me if I could see how my feet moved, how my hands moved and how high I was jumping. I replied that I could. He asked if I could imagine what the rim felt like in when my hands touched the metal, I said yes.

He then told me to visualize that into my reality, he taught me to change my mindset, how to manifest. Each night when I was in bed before I would go to sleep, I was supposed to visualize myself dunking the basketball over and over again until I fell asleep, better than counting sheep jumping over a fence, laugh out loud! I did that for a whole year, each night. I practiced in the gym during the day and visualized it at night.

One year later I could dunk the basketball easily and I entered into my first televised dunking contest at the age of sixteen.

Story Two

When I was 15 years old, my biggest dream was to go and play basketball in the US. I had just started playing basketball and I was considered a very promising player, but not good yet.

All I could think about was to go to America. At 16, in 1993, I got a friend of mine who has ties to the US to help me make a basketball reel of me doing drills on the basketball court, supervised and directed by him. He was experienced in helping basketball players get into US schools. We sent the tape to a few high schools, and I got selected to go to a high school in Pennsylvania where a very nice family decided to host me.

My dream was about to become real. I bought the plane ticket, but 2 weeks before my departure, the family contacted me and said they were so sorry but due to family issues, they could no longer accommodate me.

I was shocked and sad. But I kept on thinking about playing in the US, that's all I wanted. Each time I thought about it I felt great, like it had already happened. Every time I thought about playing basketball in the US, I got butterflies in my stomach. At that time I did not know anything about the law of attraction, but that does not matter, because I, as all of us, use the law each day by the selection of thoughts and by how much emotion is put behind each thought.

With my dream on hold, I played basketball in Iceland and did really well, started to become a decent player and won several gold medals with my team there. I started to look at junior colleges trying to find a way to go to America and play basketball, I was obsessed with my dream. At this point in time I just knew I was going to play in the US but I did not know how.

In the spring of 1997 I went with the junior national team to play in Sweden in an international basketball tournament. I was scouted by a coach from Norway who wanted me to come and play with his team that fall.

He was a former US college basketball coach and told me he would help me get to the US if I would come and play with his team. I was very excited. I took the contract home with me, which I, and my parents as witnesses, signed.

However, sometimes the law of attraction works in a strange way, and here is an example of how, in July 1997 I was ready to send the contract to Norway, buy a ticket and move there, when I got a surprising phone call from my friend who tried to help me in 1993 with the basketball reel.

He told me that a coach he knew in the US wanted two players from Iceland to come and join his team and get a full scholarship at the university for four years. Why was he willing to offer a full scholarships to players he had not even seen in person?

In the beginning of the summer 1997 the former basketball coach at Campbellsville University had a heart attack and died. Travis Ford, became the new head coach at the university, but it was so late in the summer that he had few options to recruit players.

He decided to call a friend of his in Iceland, my friend as well, and ask him for help. He still had two full scholarships to give out but having gotten the coaching position so late in the summer forced him to rely on the word of our mutual friend. I contacted the coach in Norway and told him it was my dream to play in the US and I was going for it. He understood that and congratulated me.

I flew to the states in August 1997 and experienced my dream. I was living my dream. I experienced for the first time what great coaches can do for you, they take you to the next level you would not reach on your own. The coaches at the university were top notch and because I have great work ethics, I was in the best shape of my life. I am so grateful today for my 5 years in Kentucky, both for the highs and lows. I graduated from Campbellsville University, with a bachelor's degree in business administration, in 2002.

This is how the law of attraction works in a nutshell, you can never know how exactly you attract things into your life. I am not saying I had anything to do with the heart attack.

However if you think about your goals most of the time, with a great feeling and positive emotions, the universe will deliver exactly that to you, often in the most unexpected way, exactly at the right time.

Repelling Your Dream

Since we are talking about success, why must include what not to do. If there is anything in your life right now that you don't want and are trying to manifest a change, but it seems to fail every time you try. Then the most likely reason is because you are focusing on your "not want's". What you focus on is what you attract.

If you are tired of all the bills and are thinking about not having bills, more bills will be attracted to you, because of the energy state you live in. If you want to start attracting the opposite you need to reverse your focus into the opposite. What is opposite of bills? Wealth, abundance, cash flow, money, income-streams and so forth. Focus on what you want in life, that's how you get more of it.

You are Using the Law of Attraction Daily

Have you ever known for a fact something that you have not done already, something that will occur in the future, something you are 100% sure of, but not necessarily sure how it will occur?

Let's take a very simple example. Your car is not working and the bus is not running this day that you wake up and you need to go to the store, the store is about one hour walking distance from your home and you usually drive or take the bus, these two options are not available that day, but you know 100% for a fact that you will find a way to get to the store, you are so sure that you have the wallet ready, your made your grocery list and you have that letter ready you are going to put into the mailbox at the store.

You might be thinking reading this, this is too simple, I will just walk to the store even if it takes one hour to get there and one hour back. You are 100% right again, this is what we do with your dreams. If you can use this certainty to visualize your dream, your will attract it into your reality, knowing you can always just walk there.

If you can think about the dream and know for a fact that it will come true, you will get it, but remember you might have to walk there.

Dreams take a lot of emotions and energy to reach, but you can make sure you experience them all by knowing for a fact that they all will come true. Do you want to know the shortcut to realize your dream even sooner? Of course you do. The shortcut is to do the following 4 things daily.

Once you BELIEVE, anything becomes possible! Once you KNOW, failing becomes impossible!

- Huni Hunfjord.

Your Daily Ritual.

Firstly.

Write out your dream and describe all the details as much as you can, write who you are thanking, write what clothes you are wearing in the future when you are thanking someone for the help they gave you, on your way towards your dream. Write what you are smelling that day and how you are smelling.

Write what you are hearing, what you feel on your skin, what type of clothes are you wearing, what does the fabric feel like on your skin. Write what the temperature is like in the room you are in, or outside if you are outside. Write who is thanking you. Write how blessed you are on that day. The more details you can write each day the more powerful the visualization will become and the more accurate it will unfold. Write and while you write feel it and experience it as it is already done.

Secondly.

Talk it into existence. Talk to someone about your dream, tell them everything. This is a very thin ice to walk on, because you have to choose your audience very carefully. My advice is to talk only about your dreams with more successful people in the beginning, while you might still have some room for doubt. Talking to others about your dreams, make them even more real.

You should speak with enthusiasm like it's already done. You energy should be such that people can't tell if you have done it already or not. You should be passionate about the topic, which I already know you are. This process will magnify the effect of writing your dream into existence.

This process might surprise you because this might be what actually manifests your dream. If you tell the right person about your dream, he or she might be looking to partner up with a person like you or even want to invest in you or know someone that can help you get started.

Most people who are already successful have two positive aspects that benefit you in sharing your vision and dreams.

Firstly they will not discourage you because they have already been down that road and secondly, most of them got their first opportunity by someone else believing in them. They might want to pay it forward. Make sure though that they want to hear it! Don't force this on anyone, but tell them if they ask you about it, then go for it.

Thirdly.

Visualize this several times per day by experiencing the dream already true. You can easily do this by setting your alarm clock for every two hours of your waking time, while you get used to this idea.

Once the alarm goes off, take 15-30 seconds to close your eyes and feel all the things you wrote down that morning about your dream already being true, get into the state of euphoria while seeing and hearing in your mind all the wonderful things this dream will do for you and your family and friends.

Your emotions are the energy signals you send out to the universal consciousness and it will bring you exactly the same kind of energy back.

Fourthly.

Become the person who you describe you will be once you have your dream come true. Will you be different? Will you dress different then? Will you chew your food different?

Will you smile differently? Will you shake people's hands differently than now? Will you talk differently? Will you walk differently? Will you straighten you back out and walk as tall as possible, with authority? Whatever you will become in your vision, become that right now, today!

Yes, you read this right, become the person who you visualize in the future, right now.

As a matter of fact if you dress differently, then put this book down right now and change clothes. You transformation is already on its way, even faster than you expect.

As soon as you picked up your copy of our book and decided to read it, you decided to be more and you will. You are!

Summary

- Write your vision into existence with passion

- Talk your vision into existence with passion and emotion

- Close your eyes and experience it already done, several times per day

- Become the person you will become then, NOW, and that's how your dreams come true

5. Effective First Impression

Effective First Impression.

Making a great lasting first impression will help you develop personal as well as business relationships and make easy friends and sales. From the moment you talk to a person, your behavior, attitude and personal presentation will influence people to become friends or a customer that will buy or not.

It takes just a blink of an eye, maybe a few seconds, for someone to check you when you meet them for the first time. In this very short time, the other person forms an opinion about you based on your appearance, your body language, your behavior, your gestures, and how you are dressed.

With every new person you meet, you are evaluated and yet another person's impression of you is formed.

These very important first impression can be nearly impossible to reverse or change, making those first encounters tremendously important, for they set the tone for all the relationships that follows.

So, whether they are in your career or social life, it's important to know how to create a positive first impression. Here a few tips.

Be on Time

A person you are meeting for the first time is definitely not interested in your "good excuse" for showing up late.

Make sure to arrive a few minutes early. Leave on time to make it on time. Allow flexibility for possible delays in traffic or taking a wrong turn. Arriving early is much better that arriving late, hands down, and is the first step in creating a great first impression.

Be Yourself, Be at Ease

If you are feeling stressed and on edge, this can make the other person ill at ease and that's a sure way to create a bad unprofessional impression. If you are relaxed and assertive, so the other person will feel more at ease, and you will have a solid foundation for making that first impression a great one.

How to Present Yourself

Of course, the way you look matters. The person you are meeting for the first time does not know you and your appearance is normally the first clue about you.

But it certainly does not mean you need to look like you just did the catwalk to create a strong, positive first impression. No. The key to a good impression is to present yourself appropriately.

They say a picture is worth a thousand words, and so the "picture" you first present to them says much about you. Is your appearance saying the correct things to help create the good healthy first impression?

Let's start with the way you dress. What is the appropriate dress for the meeting or occasion? In a business setting, what is the appropriate business attire? Suit, blazer or maybe casual?

And ask yourself what the person you'll be meeting is likely to wear? If your contact is in marketing or the entertainment industry, a pinstripe business suit may not strike the right note!

For business and social meetings, appropriate clothing also varies between countries and cultures, so it's something that you should pay particular attention to when in an unfamiliar setting or country. Make sure you know the traditions, culture and values.

And what about you're grooming? A clean (shaved) and tidy appearance is appropriate for most business and social occasions. A good haircut. Clean and tidy clothes. Appropriate and tidy makeup. Make sure your grooming is appropriate and helps make you feel good and fit-in.

Appropriate clothing and grooming will create a good first impression and also help you feel relaxed and so feel more calm and confident. All of this together and you are well on your way to creating a fantastic lasting first impression.

Good news is you can usually create a good impression without total losing your individuality. Sure, to make a good first impression you do need to make sure you fit-in to some degree. But it all goes back to being appropriate for the situation. If in a business setting, wear appropriate business attire.

If at a formal social evening event, wear appropriate evening attire and express your individuality correctly within that context.

Have the Best Smile!

"Smile and the world smiles too" is a common saying. So there's nothing like a great smile to create a fantastic first impression. A warm, honest and confident smile will put both at ease. Smiling is a winner when it comes to great first impressions but don't go overboard with this. People who take this too far can seem insincere and creepy, or can be seen to be "lightweights."

Be Open and Confident

Make that first appearance one they will remember. When it comes to making the first good impression, body language as well as appearance speaks much louder than any words.

Use your body language to project appropriate confidence and self-assurance. Stand tall, smile, make eye contact, greet with a firm confident handshake. This will help you project confidence and encourage both you and the other person to feel better at ease.

Most of us will get a little nervous when meeting someone for the first time, which can lead to nervous habits or sweaty palms. By being aware of your nervous habits, you can try to control them. Controlling a nervous jitter or a nervous laugh will give you confidence and help the other person feel at ease.

Small talk goes a very long way.

Normally all conversations are based on verbal give and take. It may help you to prepare questions you have for the person you are meeting for the first time beforehand so you are not losing your cool.

If you like you can also take a few minutes to learn something about the person you meet for the first time before you get together. For instance, does he like sports? Does she work with a local organization?

Is there anything that you know of, that you have in common with the person you are meeting? If so, this can be a great way to open the conversation and to keep it moving forward.

Be Positive

Be sure you are positive instead of negative. Your attitude shines through in everything you do. Project a positive firm attitude, even in the face of criticism or in the case of nervousness.

Learn from your meeting and to contribute properly, maintaining an optimistic manner and a smile. There are many things upsetting your business that you can't control.

Your own attitude is something you can control. Your attitude affects the way you approach people and events in business.

Choosing to approach potential customers positively, confidently, enthusiastically and with a helpful attitude, even when you're tired, stressed or not happy, will improve your sales performance and improve your sales results.

Remember that every business exists to meet the customer's needs. Believing that your job is to solve and understand your customers needs and problems, will boost your natural and helpful confidence.

Be Courteous and Attentive

We all know that good manners and polite, attentive and courteous behavior help make a good first impression. Anything less can decay the one chance you have at making that first great impression so be on your best behavior.

Make sure to turn off your mobile phone, not vibration mode only or whatever else you plan on doing, just turn it off. Make sure all attention goes to the person you are meeting for the first time? Your new acquaintance deserves 100% of your attention.

Anything less than that and you'll create a less than good first impression. There are no second chances of a first impression.

Personal Presentation

Your appearance shows your customer that you respect them, your business, products and services. Here are some useful personal presentation tips:

- Have a straight posture, confident and relaxed.

- Don't distract your customer with personal things while talking to them. They are not interested.

- Take care over your choice of dress, and tailor your wardrobe to appeal to your customer base. Dress to impress.

- Make sure your hair as well as your nails are well-groomed.

The Key Points

You only have a few seconds to make a healthy first impression and it's almost impossible to change this impression so it's worth giving each new encounter your best shot.

Most of what you need to do to make a great impression is based on common sense, but with a little extra thought and preparation, you can make every first impression not just good but a great first impression.

6. Who is BOB?

Who is BOB?

In this chapter it might be good for you to tone down the language for the young souls listening if you are reading this to your children or language sensitive folks.

I usually don't curse because I think it's unnecessary most of the time but when it comes to fucking BOB, we must cross that line. Who the fuck is this BOB? Why the fuck do we need to be afraid all the time? Why are we being held back?

Let me tell you why, it's because BOB loves you so fucking much. BOB was put into the human race thousands of years ago.

BOB was put into humans to protect them. He protected our ancestors from walking off a cliff, walking into the open mouth of a saber tooth tiger and even from trying new foods, new berries or anything not known to be safe. We lived in caves and traveled outside the cave as little as possible to survive.

We knew the cave was safe, it became what we know today as the comfort zone, where you can relax, unbuttoning you tight jeans and let your farts out without a silencer and not worrying about being eaten by saber tooth tiger who heard your loud fart.

When we are about to do something for the first time, BOB is screaming of the top of his lungs inside your head "YOU ARE GONNA DIE", do you recognize that feeling? Sure you do, remember that time when you had to talk in front of a crowd the first time and you actually felt like you were about to die!

Do you remember when you did something that scared you so much while it was still your first something, like first day at school, first day at the new job, first something?

It's funny when you think about it now, because now, you have mastered it. You have arrived at work every day for the last 10 years and you could probably do your job half way asleep by now, while during the first day you felt like you were about to die.

BOB is always trying to protect you and your job from now on is to recognize this, when this is happening and realize that this is a mechanism to keep you alive. Once you have evaluated the situation with your knowledge of BOB, then you will find out that there is no reason to fear death in that particular situation, just put BOB in the back seat of your vehicle, strap him in and go on.

BOB is your protector but he is paranoid as hell. He will trigger emotions that will derail your mission if you allow him to that, if you allow him to sit in the front he will pull the steering wheel and derail the locomotive. Do not under any circumstances allow him in the front, you are stuck with BOB so the best thing is to strap him in tightly in the back and keep going.

Back to Square One

Have you ever experienced or seen other people, that once they reach a goal, they snap back to square one, self-sabotage their success? A great example would be weight loss.

A person sets a goal to lose 20 pounds and succeeds. When they succeed, they let go and gain 22 pounds back, making them 2 pounds heavier than before they started working towards their original goal.

Have you seen this happen or maybe even experienced it yourself? Do you know why this happens?

It's because when you reach that goal you let BOB in the front seat. It's because when you reach the goal or even sometimes when you are getting close to achieving that goal you might self-sabotage the results you have already achieved.

The reason is that BOB thinks you are standing at the end of the world, metaphorically speaking, on the edge. You are on the edge of the known heading into the unknown. BOB does not know what is next. You only have this one goal and when you reach it, you are living in the zone of the unknown. What's next? How can you avoid this?

How can you prevent BOB from screaming in your head "YOU ARE GONNA DIE, GO BACK TO THE KNOWN", which in this case is being at least 20 pounds overweight.

To prevent this from happening you will have to set yourself two goals each time, at least. Two steps in front of you.

We don't want to let BOB into the front seat, he is a lousy driver. We don't want to create a ledge of the unknown.

So you are going to set yourself at least two goals from now on and when you are close to reaching the first one, then you need to set the next goal, because you always need two steps in front of while you are walking the ladder of success. At least two steps, two goals, remember that! To ensure that you do not let BOB take over you need to know what BOB stands for and have two goals, or two steps.

Consider all of this, next time you get that uncomfortable feeling, next time you feel so bad about doing something new that you feel nauseated and you might feel like you are going to die if you proceed, then think about the worst case, best case and most likely case. Count to three and make a decision, GO!

Do it with your fear in the back, keep BOB in line, he should not be allowed to get so close the steering wheel that he will affect the outcome.

If you can't control BOB, if you cannot take control, if you can't put him in the back of your vehicle then there is an alternative solution for you. Take BOB and make him bigger! Yes use your fear in the right way. Be more afraid of not growing.

Be more afraid of meeting the possible future version of yourself, the one you could have become by taking that chance, doing that speech, writing that book or whatever it is that scares you now.

Be more afraid of quitting, more afraid of shrinking into a small ball and slowly dying, because you are pure energy and energy is never still. Remember that! Be more afraid of not growing than ever what is going to happen if you take that change, if you jump now!

You are either growing or dying. Be more afraid to die in regret. Find what works the best for you. Putting BOB in the back or making him bigger!

Summary

- BOB is your fear

- BOB keeps you safe

- BOB loves you

- BOB is over protective of you and limits you!

- Set two goals, two steps in front of you all the time so BOB will stay in the back seat of your vehicle

- If you can't control BOB, use reverse psychology and make him bigger, be more afraid of not trying and dying in regret than trying.

7. Step Up to Success

Step Up to Success

Why do we look back so much? We are not going that way. Let's start moving and looking forward where all the opportunities are. Let's go for success and happiness. Stop pointing fingers because every time you point a finger, 3 are pointing at yourself. Are you ready for the future? YES, and I am also willing to help the people who want this as well.

You have the power to become that great hero, that successful entrepreneur. It all starts with a choice. Start by believing in yourself and start seeing the reality. Nothing comes from words alone. It always needs tons of action to get results and this is an ongoing process, luck is something you will eventually run out off, for sure.

Only hard work alone will only get you so far. Hard and smart is not the same, it's a totally different story. Knowledge is potential power and with the correct attitude this package is bound for mega success.

Discipline yourself to do what you know you need to do, to be the very best in your field.

What is self-discipline?

Perhaps the best description of self-discipline is that self-discipline is the ability to make yourself do what you need to do, when you need to do it, whether you feel like it or not. It is easy to do something when you simply feel like it.

Now when you don't feel like it and you force yourself to do it anyway that is how you move your life and career onto the fast track.

What real decisions do you need to make in order to start moving toward the top of your field? Whatever it is, either to get in or get out, make a decision today and then get started. This single act alone can change your life forever.

Are You Ready

Why is it that many people fail to reach success, when there is so many statistics showing them how to be successful? Find out how your habits effect the success or failure you achieve.

People living today are extremely lucky.

When I was young the internet did not exist and cable TV was something you read about in a science fiction magazines. In my home we had a black and white TV with two channels and the only thing on TV in the evening was the news. Now, thanks to the internet, you can find information on virtually anything you want, instantly. Something which was only a dream just one decade ago today.

With all this information available to us, many people still fail to become successful in life. Why is this? After all, there is so much information available showing us how to be successful, but most people still fail to achieve any success. Why do people still suffer from depression, when there are so many books and media outlets telling them how to live a great, healthy and positive life?

It is very simple, information is not the problem and no matter how much technology advances, people will always have the same problems.

Reasons for Failure

If you ask a person why they never succeeded in what they were trying to do, they will most likely tell you it was not their fault, or something happened that was beyond their control.

If you compare that person's life against someone else's life, you could probably find many instances of people who suffered under much harder conditions yet still became very successful.

This shows us that the real reason people fail is not because of something outside of them, rather the reason lies within them.

When you keep doing the same thing over and over again it is called a habit. You are almost certainly familiar with bad habits such as smoking, drinking or biting nails but are you familiar with the habits of failure or the habits of success?

Habits of Success

Success or failure is ultimately achieved through the actions you take, habits therefore play a remarkable role in determining whether you will achieve great success or failure in life. If you read every day, it is a habit.

This habit is likely to expand your knowledge on a specific subject or matter, and vastly improve the chances you will master it and be successful at it.

Instead of reading every day, many people prefer to sit down and watch TV for a few hours. Do you think this will help master any subject or become an expert in your field? In all likelihood, the answer will be no.

So if you look at accomplishing success or failure in terms of the actions you repeat on a daily basis, then it is quite simple to understand why some people succeed, and others complain about failure. People who are successful continually do things on a daily basis that will increase their chances of success whilst unsuccessful people do not and they will often complain about there situation to justify their inaction's to others.

This does not mean successful people never fail, because they do fail, but what they don't do, is to give up, because they have developed habits of success.

Change Your Habits

The message I try to share is that in order to experience change in your life you must first identify your habits.

Think about what do you do every day and ask yourself if those things help you achieve what you want in life?

If the answer is no, you must change those habits, because by doing the same thing over and over again you will get the same results over and over again.

Achieving your goals towards success is done by taking one step at the time.

Make Your Dreams Reality

Let's imagine that it is real. Try to see every detail so clearly that you can reach out and touch it. You can feel the emotions? For example, if you want an amazing motorcycle, then what type is it? What brand is it? What color is it? Imagine you are sitting on it like you will when it is brand new. How does it feel? How does it sounds? Go for a drive on your motorcycle in your mind. WAUUUW!

Experience the wind blowing in your face. Hear the sounds around you. If you can take a real test drive in one, do that!

Get a picture of your dream bike and place it where you will see it each and every day. Do this visualization several times a day until it becomes part of you. This action is important because your subconscious will help enable you to reach your goals to achieve your dream.

Next, break the big dream down into precise, assessable goals to get you there. If you are dreaming of something that costs a certain amount of money, like the motorcycle, you will set a specific date on when you want to have the money saved up for the bike.

Once you have your date, then break your timeline down into segments. Perhaps you set the date nine months from now. So the next step is to break that down into a goal for each month, then a goal for each week, then a goal for each day. It may be easier to start with the days, and then multiply out to the weeks and months, BOOOM and it's there already, congrats, you look so good on the new bike.

Now that you know what your specific timeline looks like, you need to determine the specific actions you can take to reach each specific goal.

If it is a financial goal, like what we talked about before, you know how much money you need to put aside each day. So now you need to find out what actions you need to take each day in order to be able to do that for real.

If your goal is accomplishing a new project, your timeline will be broken down into different steps you need to finish in order to get the whole project done.

So the first big accomplishment on your way to that goal is to complete the proper relevant research. Then you need to set a time to complete your elementary outline. Then a time to complete each part. Then a time for editing. You can break each step down into smaller steps that must be done each day in order to complete the entire project by your target date.

Now that you see what you will need to do each day in order to achieve your big goal, ask yourself if each day's task is reasonable.

Be honest with yourself. If you know you can do what is needed each day, then you have your plan.

If it will be extremely difficult to accomplish each day's requirement, then extend your timeline until you have something you know you can get done every day. This way, you are setting yourself up for sure success!

It is this simple, "A journey of a thousand miles begins with one step." No matter how big your dreams are, if you break it down into mini steps that you can do each day, you will find your road to success filled with happiness of achieving many goals.

Reaching even a small goal will, indeed, assure you that you are on your way to reaching your big dream! You will gain the confidence you need to continue and to receive what you desire, you need to do whatever actions are required each day!

Have a good time with achieving even the little goals, and enjoy your road to your certain success!

Believe in Yourself

Your ideals in life determine what you believe, about yourself and the world around you, your reality. If you have positive believes, such as love, compassion, and generosity, you will believe that people in your world are deserving of these virtues and you will treat them accordingly to your believes.

When you believe in yourself and chose to be a better person with every day passing, you will find yourself to be more happy, positive and successful in life.

Know Your Values in Life

Your beliefs, in turn, regulate the third ring of your personality, your hopes. If you have positive values, you will believe yourself to be a great person. If you believe in yourself to be a good person, you will expect good things to come your way. If you expect good things to come to you, you will be positive, happy and open for a bright future and ready to receive it into your reality when it presents itself to you.

You will look for the greatness in other people in different situations and with practice bring that greatness out in them.

Attitude

Your attitude will project outwards the image of your values, beliefs, and hopes. If your value is that, this is a good world to live in and your belief is that you are going to be very successful in life, you will expect and experience that everything that happens to you is helping you in some way. You will identify it's purpose, each time.

As a result, you will have a positive mental attitude toward other people and they will return that positive attitude toward you. You will be a happy and optimistic person that others will notice. You will be someone who others want to hang around or work with and for, do business with, and generally help to become more successful.

Be a Good Person

Your actions on the outside will ultimately reflect your values, beliefs, and hopes on the inside.

This is why what you achieve in life and work will be determined more by what is going on inside of you than by any other external factors.

Action Exercise

Make a list of your most important values in life today. What do you really believe in and stand for? Make the list as long as you want because these are your values.

What are your most important values in life? What qualities are you best known for among your friends and family? What do you see as the most important values guiding your relationships with others in your life?

Expect and wish for good things to happen and work hard towards your goals and you will find yourself living a happy and successful life, sooner rather than later.

8. Get over it and celebrate

Breaking Mental Blocks and Celebrating Wins

Break down your blocks and start your transformation toward your goals. Do you actively seek advice from people who are more successful than you? Are you implementing all the things that you are reading and learning from someone who has done it before?

It is important to know why you might not have been taken action in the past. It is possible that you have a mental block, a subconscious block or like some people like to call it, a limiting belief. That is basically something you decided to believe at some point in time that has been limiting you and holding you back. Many people do not know why they did not start implementing routines of success in their lives and maybe this information will help you get started, as I know it sure did pole vault my success forward. Let's start with three questions, please only provide yes or no answers.

Are you seeking to grow and become more than you are today?

Do you want to become a better person?

Have you ever wanted more out of life than you have now e.g. success, career, relationship, money or anything else?

If you answered all three questions with a yes, then you are in the right place. Now one more question, but before I ask, let me tell you one thing; it takes action and some willpower to transform your life.

When you answer this question, say the answer out loud as it makes it easier for you to monitor how you are truly feeling. It's very important to monitor the vibrational changes in your body when you answer. Here is the question.

Do you truly want to transform your life in any way, become a better person, be better off financially, have better relationships, be happier or anything else that you would like to transform?

If you said yes, did you notice anything?

What did you notice when you answered the question out loud?

Did you get a feeling of release from the upper body, did you open up and feel very good?

If you did you are most likely already starting to transform your life in some way or already have everything you ever wanted. But maybe you had a gut feeling that what you said is true but something is not quite right. That gut feeling is one of the most important tools we are born with, to tell us if the conscious and subconscious mind is working in alignment or not. Our conscious beliefs might be the opposite of what we subconsciously truly believe, for whatever reason that might be.

If you said yes to the last question but had a gut feeling that something was off, you most likely have what is called a subconscious block. That could easily be the reason that you have not yet taken the required action in the transformation you would like to see in your life.

A subconscious block is when your beliefs trigger an emotional response to a certain situation and that emotion could be fear for example, good old BOB protecting you, like he always does. (see chapter 6. Who is BOB?)

If you have already started your journey in your transformation, this method can be useful for you, for other subconscious blocks that you might have or might encounter in the future.

This is one of many methods to unlock the subconscious belief that is blocking you. In this example we are going to be concentrating on those who got the gut feeling that something was not quite right, because it could possibly be the reason you have not transformed your life already, or taken the right action needed to start your transformation.

This exercise can undo the subconscious block you have and remember this can be used on any type of subconscious blocks you might have. You must ask this question over and over again, what is it that I am not satisfied with, what has not turned out like I wanted it to be and ask what possible belief could a person have to encountered this situation (or lack off), you are thinking about right now?

Keep asking and answering it again and again, what could a person belief to cause this recurring unwanted result?

When you answer this question correctly you who body will feel it and you will probably say something like this to yourself, "Holy cow, that's why it is what it is".

When I personally did this exercise I found myself to belief that I would have to do everything myself, I worked on it and overcame it and now I am co-writing this book plus I have several hundred contracting jobs completed since then. Now you might belief that you cannot change and that's why you haven't and we are going to use that as an example in this chapter. Your subconscious belief might be that you cannot change your life, so let's change that with this simple exercise.

Change Your Subconscious Belief.

Please take out a piece of paper and a pen.

Write this down on the paper; "My old belief, I cannot transform my life."

Then write the opposite statement below the first statement; "My new true belief, I can and I will transform my life."

Then when you have time, find a quiet room with the lights dimmed. Turn your cell phone off and anything that can cause interruption.

Now relax yourself into a meditative state, for those who meditate on a regular basis know what that is and for those who do not, this is how.

Take deep breaths, relaxing and calming your body down and concentrate on each body part, head, face, neck, shoulders, arms, hands, chest, stomach, back, legs and feet. Focus on each body part, moving from your head to your toes and feel the relaxation when you focus on each body part.

Next you calm the mind by thinking about a single word, you could use the word "love" for example or any other word you would like. Thinking about this one word will help your mind to relax. Those who meditate use their mantras to do the same.

When you feel your mind relaxed then say the following statement out loud, as soft and effortless as possible, your ears should be able to hear it but no louder than that.

"Hi, my subconscious mind.

Up until now we have been holding on to this old belief that I cannot transform my life.

I now realize that this belief is false. I want you to replace that old belief that I cannot transform my life, with this new true belief which is; I can and I will transform my life. From this day forward we will replace the old false belief that I cannot transform my life, with this new true belief that I can and I will transform my life.

I want you to permanently replace this old false belief that I cannot transform my life, with this new true belief that I can and I will transform my life, permanently. Make it so now and forever!"

Repeat that statement for 5, 10, 20 minutes or however long it will take to release you block. You will feel when this is done, when you transform the vibration of your subconscious mind there will be no doubt, you will feel it, you will know it.

When this is done don't forget to thank your subconscious mind like you would thank an old friend for good advice or how you would thank someone that wants to invest in you.

If for any reason the old belief surfaces in the next two weeks, be alert and catch it right away. Say this out loud and laugh at it. "No I don't believe that anymore now I have this new true belief that I can and I will transform my life." This will shift your energy vibration back into alignment right then and there.

Here is the really good news, when you have done this you're halfway there.

I honestly believe that this is the case with anything we do in life. Take the first step and you are halfway there. The reason I chose this method to teach you here, is because it worked and works the best for me.

I want to congratulate you on completing this first step and here is a small bonus tip for you to accelerate your growth even faster using this method or any other for that matter.

Have you ever heard of Richard Branson? Let me tell you one thing that he does and I do as well today. Each time Richard Branson has a small success of any kind he celebrates it in some way. Each time I reach a goal today, even a small success on the treadmill, I celebrate.

Find something that gives you a rewarding feeling, it could be anything, like going to the movies, out for a dinner, cooking with the family, taking a drive through the countryside with the family, or simply reaching your arms up in the air like you just won the marathon at the Olympics, whatever makes you feel like a winner.

Use this thing to celebrate each little win or progress you make.

Summary

- To start taking action, we have to find what is stopping us. That reason why we have not taken action before is most often a subconscious block or in other words a belief we might not have realized we had.

- Take that subconscious block, reverse it and create a new subconscious belief.

- Celebrate each little victory in life. Stop and smell the roses!

THE TIME TO START YOUR TRANSFORMATION IS NOW!

9. Mind Power

"What we are today comes from our thoughts of yesterday, and our present thoughts build our life of tomorrow: Our life is the creation of our mind."

- Buddha

Achieve Goals Using Mind Power

All bodily reality is made up of vibrations of energy, even your thoughts are brain vibrations of energy. Maybe it sounds like a concept or hard theory, this is a new reality that quantum physics has revealed to us. Your thoughts have a powerful influence on your life and the people around you.

You're Thoughts

Most of us go through life taking little notice of our thinking processes. How the mind works, what it fears, what it notices, what it says to itself, what it clashes aside. For the most part, we go about your lives with hardly any attention on how we think.

We go through life overlooking one of the most important and powerful forces in our life, our thoughts.

Your Focus

Your mind is directing your thoughts towards a desired outcome in your life. Focus on success and you will attract success. Focus on fear and failure and you attract just that. This is the circle of the mind.

The power of your mind is understanding these principles and making your thoughts work for you. Any thoughts are the primary creative forces in your life. Use them wisely and you will awaken to a whole new life of power and opportunity.

A New Life

To make changes in your life, your must change. You must change the way you use your mind. Both negative and positive thoughts at the same time are not possible, as one will always control the other. As humans, we are creatures of habits, and so is your mind. You must make sure to think empowering thoughts and have positive emotions with those thoughts which are the dominating your mind.

Change Both Ways

Many people forget this huge important step.

If you try to change some conditions by simply working directly on those conditions, it will almost always proves pointless, unless it is done side by side with a change of thoughts and beliefs.

Train your conscious mind to think happy thoughts of opportunities, success, health, and prosperity. Learn to take out negativity such as fear and worry. Keep your conscious mind busy with the expectation of the best and make sure the thoughts you think are based upon what you truly want in your life.

The Subconscious Mind.

We all have a subconscious mind, but for most of us, our knowledge of it is very limited. Your subconscious mind is a hidden mind that exists within you and controls many things behind the scene.

Think of your subconscious mind as incredibly fertile soil that will grow any seed you plant in it. Think of it as your garden. Your repeated thoughts and beliefs are seeds that are being regularly sown into the garden and they will eventually turn flowers or trees in your garden, so make sure to pick them carefully.

Just as apple tree produce apples, the contents of your thoughts will have an effect in your life. You will reap what you sow, this we cannot change, but what you sow you can change.

Your conscious mind is your garden. It's your responsibility to be aware of how this process works and choose wisely what reaches the inner garden (your subconscious) and is being sown. For most of us, our role as the gardener has never been explained. By not knowing this role, we have allowed seeds of all types to enter our subconscious mind, our garden.

The subconscious doesn't distinguish, judge, or censor. It obeys your commands which are your thoughts and emotions together. It will manifest success, happiness, abundance, and health just as easily as failure, sickness, and misfortune. Your subconscious accepts what is impressed upon it with feeling and repetition, whether these thoughts are positive or negative, so chose them wisely.

It does not evaluate things like your conscious mind does. This is why it is so important to be aware of what you are thinking.

Synchronicity

Now you understand that your subconscious will bring you what you need or desire, through what you project with your thoughts and emotions on a daily base. Now you need to select your thoughts based on what you truly want and things will start happening for you.

To the untrained mind, synchronicity appears to be a coincidence or just luck. It is neither. It is simply the operation of the forces you have set into motion with your thoughts and emotions.

This strong mechanism that you possess, like the rest of humanity, works with your conscious mind. It will bring to you the people and circumstances you require to achieve your goals.

Modern physics sees the universe as a cosmic, inseparable web of energetic activity. Not only is the universe alive and constantly changing, but everything in the universe affects everything else.

We now know that everything in the universe is made up of energy. Everything from the items in your house, to the events that happen to you and the people around you, and even our thoughts are made up of vibrations of energy.

This means our thoughts are made of the exact same substance as the building masses of the universe. Knowing this, we can use it to our benefit.

Before, it might have seemed unbelievable that we could create our reality through this process.

But now you know how to do it and why it works. Since your thoughts are energy, it only makes sense that frequent images, confirmations, deeply held beliefs, fears and strong needs will have an effect on your reality by vibrating within the wast reality which is made of other energy vibrations.

With these fields of energy colliding all over, we are all connected. We are all connected though the universal consciousness, where all the energy fields collide or merge.

Visualizations

We live in an immense ocean of vibrating energy that responses to how and what we think. Our thoughts are creative forces and are constantly expressing themselves in our lives. Once we realize this, we can begin designing our lives with a clear purpose.

So how can you use this reality in your life? By focusing daily on what you desire, your wants. The first stage is visualization.

Visualizing is simply a mental preparation for things to come. You create images in your mind of having or doing whatever it is that you want. You then repeat these images over and over again, daily as often as you feel like it. The more often you do it the faster it works for you.

The key to visualizing is to always visualize you already having what you are manifesting into your life. This is a mental trick. Rather than hoping you will achieve it, or building confidence that one day it might happen, live and feel it as if it has already happened to you now.

You know this is just a mental trick, but the subconscious mind cannot distinguish between what is real and what is only your imagination. Your subconscious will act upon the pictures you create within based on the feeling you provide with them, whether they reflect your current reality or not. It's not magic, and it doesn't happen overnight, but if you persist in your vision, you will be successful before you know it.

Whatever your definition as your success, you can achieve it.

You can achieve anything you put your mind to, once you understand the power of your mind.

Affirmations

Affirmations are statements that you either say out loud, or silently to yourself. By doing this, you affirm to yourself whatever it is that you desire. For example, if you have an important interview coming up, you could affirm to yourself that you will have a great interview and the outcome.

When you speak something and repeat it to yourself, it will influence your thoughts. This is why affirmations are so successful.

If you say to yourself that you will have a great interview, your mind will automatically begin to look for all the signs to approach the interview as a great interview. You will go in there with the attitude of already having the job, that gives your a totally different energy vibration and the person or people interviewing you will feel it.

What you focus on, grows or so to speak, so start using affirmations to focus on what you want.

Avoid negative or disappointing question that might lead to a bad interview. Those kind of questions might lead to being extremely nervous in the interview. These words focus on the opposite of what you want. Be positive, strong and use words that reflect what you truly want. If you want to be confident, use that word in your affirmation daily leading up to that interview.

Use a short slogan, or one sentence at the most. Your affirmation should be like a simple chant that you can repeat over and over again, without thinking too much about it. You could have something that you wake up to. Example affirmations to wake up to are, anything is possible or doors will open up for me today or people will be attracted to me today for I am a very happy human.

You don't need to force yourself to believe your affirmation, simply repeat it again and again and it will naturally have an effect on you. How many times to you have to tell yourself a lie before it becomes your truth, your new reality. What you might consider are a lie in the beginning will become your truth once you see it manifest into your reality. Making it true then. Repeating the statement will cause it to work for you and change your reality.

Affirmations are very simple, easy to use, and extremely powerful. Many professionals use them to perform well and keep their momentum going. Successful entrepreneurs use them to close deals and run their companies, and musicians use them to be creative and come up with innovative songs and music ideas. You can use them too, in any area of your life, in any way you see fit.

Acknowledging

Nothing succeeds like success, and it's true. Success vibration acts like a strong magnet that attracts more success and opportunities to you. When you think and feel success, you vibrate with the energy of success and you act accordingly.

People who are already successful have momentum on their side, the law of attraction is working for them, but then again it's working for us all, except that some of us that do not know how to use it in our advantage, we are attracting what we don't want.

Those who are already successful do attract even bigger success because of the nature of their predominant thoughts and emotions.

This vibration is a great asset to someone who is already successful or understands how this works. If you are not yet successful, no need to panic. There are many techniques to create extreme success vibration. One of them is the technique of acknowledging.

This technique begins with searching for parts of your life where you are already successful. Regrettably most of us are faster to see our own failures and inadequacies than we are to recognize our successes.

Observe your personal qualities and present situation and find things to feel gratitude for. Feel grateful for your success. Are you a good buddy to someone? Are you positive? Are you generous? Do you dress well? Don't limit your definition of success to someone who is very rich, famous, and handsome. Define your own success.

There are so many other aspects of your life that are similarly important; the key is to find aspects that help you feel successful in your own life. This is one way to create your success vibration, to raise your energy levels to be able to start receiving more of it into our life.

Start by creating a recognizing map. Your map can be either general or specific. For example, let's say you're an entrepreneur building your business. Create a specific recognizing map that highlights the qualities which will help you succeed in that role, like being a good communicator. You might have fantastic people skills. You might also recognize yourself as an amazing leader, or whatever you can think of. I am positive you have several amazing qualities.

Focusing on this list will help you create a specific success vibration. The same belief works whether you're closing a huge real estate deal, getting a new job, or finding the perfect companion.

No Negative Thinking

We already know that what you mind focus on you will attract. What you focus on grows!

Fear as well as negative thinking keeps your vibration and focus on the wrong side of success. You are thinking about what you don't want and therefore attracting more of that vibration. How can you exclude negative thinking.

Develop your mind to think about what you want in life, and avoid thinking the opposite.

Negative people as well as negative thinking drains your energy and is counterproductive. Fear is so destructive as is despair and hopelessness, you must avoid those energy frequencies as much as possible.

How do we remove this negative thinking pattern? The most important steps are to recognize the importance of removing negative thoughts and to be aware of negativity when it is happening to us. Catch it before you plant that seed into your garden.

You cannot avoid negative thinking completely. Sometimes negative thoughts just jump into our mind. When this happens, we must be mindful, so that we immediately recognize when we are thinking negatively and simply stop it.

When you catch yourselves thinking negative thoughts you can use any of these techniques:

Try to change negative thoughts into a positive thoughts.

If you're worried and focusing on what could go wrong in a situation, change your thoughts pattern to what will go right. Your mind can only think one thought at the time, so changing the negative into a positive eliminates the negative, boom. You can never think both at the same time.

By thinking before you start something for a few seconds, what's the worst that could happen, best case scenario and most likely scenario, you can eliminate a lot of unnecessary negative thoughts as you start working on your project.

Thoughts have no power at all unless you give them power. Negative thoughts gain energy when you think them over and over again. So stop thinking about already.

The key is to catch the negatives before they have time to become sprouted seeds in the garden. With practice you will notice right away when you are thinking negatively and you then can take the appropriate actions. Your mind is a creature of habit, so encourage positive thoughts and eliminate negative ones and make that your habit.

10. Your WHY

What is your WHY?

Your why is the reason you need, to be able to transform your life. The reason you use to fuel yourself and inspire yourself to achieve anything you want.

You might have read a similar statement somewhere like this one below, but what exactly does it mean?

> "Find your WHY and you're WHAT can be achieved regardless of its magnitude."

> - Huni Hunfjord

We humans have been pushing the limitations of our bodies and minds through the ages. When a person breaks a new limit, it seems like the rest of humanity can easily follow and replicate the results.

Here are two examples to explain what I mean.

The first example will describe something that we know we cannot do, or so we thought, until we do. Until the year 1954 it was thought impossible for humans to run the mile (1,609 meters) in under four minutes.

Some scientists had even published their findings, about how that was not possible due to our DNA structure and that we are simply not built to be able to run that fast. In May 1954, Roger Gilbert Bannister, was the first runner who managed to run the mile in under 4 minutes.

That in itself was amazing, but what I personally think is even more amazing, is that only two months later two other runners managed to run the mile in under 4 minutes as well. When we know something is possible, it becomes much easier to accomplish.

The second example will describe something that was unknown to this one man who changed the rules so to speak. In 1983 a potato farmer at the age of 61, won the inaugural Westfield Sydney to Melbourne Ultra marathon in Australia. This is an 875 km run. Cliff Young, the potato farmer, did not look at what other runners were doing before he ran for the first time in this race.

He did not realize that everyone would run and then sleep and then run and so forth. Because he did not know that, he ran the whole time without stopping, he did not sleep at all.

He ran for 5 days and 15 hours to finish the race and he broke the previous record by two days. From that day forward no one else slept in the race. The runners who ran the race after that knew that this was possible and they broke his record soon after that.

These two examples are to illustrate a point and for you to keep in mind. If your dream or goal in life has been accomplished by someone else, anyone, before you start your journey towards that goal, it means that it will be much easier for you to achieve the same results. You know it's been done so there is no doubt in your mind.

We continue to break our own records all the time. We know more and more about the power that we are born with inside of us that we can use, if we know how and even sometimes use without knowing that we are using it. We all have that seed of success inside of us from birth and it is so powerful, that when it awakens you will discover success beyond your wildest dreams.

How do We Unleash That Power That is Already Residing Within Us?

There are several ways of doing that. One of the most powerful methods is to find your why. To find a big enough reason to do it, so that you will be working from a higher energy frequency than before and you will continue through the tough times as well, you will not quit with a strong enough reason to do it.

The reason is so strong that your desire to finish the task at hand is unchangeable. You cannot think of anything that could stop you, except you deciding to stop. Big enough reason so that, no matter what someone else will tell you, it will not stop you on your way to achieving that goal or manifesting that dream.

If you ask yourself why, then you have to find a big reason that fires you up, that lights you up each time you think about it. Why should you become successful, why should you do better than now, why do you want it? Does it make you feel great thinking about that goal and what it will accomplish or do for you or others?

Have you ever heard a story about a mother saving her child stuck under a car and she just moves the car off the child and then she can never repeat that task? Her why at that moment was so strong, so powerful, so intense that she becomes superman or superwoman for a brief moment, wouldn't it be great to tap into that all the time!

Why is Your WHY so Important to You?

One of the biggest upsets in sports history was on February 11th in 1990 when the underdog Buster Douglas, knocked out the undisputed heavyweight champion Mike Tyson. When Buster Douglas was asked what motivated him in that fight, he explained that his mother had just passed away and during her last days on earth, she told people that Douglas would win the fight. His why was so great at the time and his win became one of the biggest upsets in sports history.

I know entrepreneurs that motivate themselves in different ways.

One of my friends shared with me that each morning when he wakes up and thinks about snoozing the alarm, he drives himself forward with the thought of, how many children can I save in the future from starvation if I just get up instead of snoozing?

He said that if he gets up and continues to grow and succeed, he will be able to give more financial support to his cause, and that is his why.

That is very powerful, but remember, his passion is helping children, around the world, who do not have enough food. That is what drives him every day, that is his why.

I have many why's, one of them is saving lives. Only three days after creating the Focus Gym ♡♡ Be you! brand I got a letter sent to me and my team. The letter was from one of our Focus Gym ♡♡ Be you! family member and she told us that she could never ever thank us enough, because the day she heard about the program she had decided to end her life. She told us that we had saved her. What an emotional reward this was for me personally and I know it was as well for the whole team.

How many more lives can we save? That is one of my big why's that drives me forward every single day.

Is Your WHY Strong Enough to Persist?

Some people say that they want to become rich and that is fine, but that is not a why. You can on the other hand use money to fulfill your why, to achieve your why. Maybe your dream is to travel the world with your family, that can be a why, but it is not a very strong one.

That means, if you have set traveling the world with your family as a why, then you must work harder than anyone you have ever seen working towards their transformation in their lives.

You will have to be one of the strongest, most motivated people on the planet to succeed with a why of that nature.

How can you find a bigger, better why? Is your why to solve hunger in the world, or to feed 1.000 people daily for the rest of your life?

Is it to leave a legacy behind for your children or maybe to empower other people to succeed in life? Maybe it is the legacy you want to leave for your children and you start working on that right now and include your children in the process.

In a few years or even 20 years from now, once you have reached your success and have a lot of money, then you might realize that money does not mean a thing. What mattered is that you left a legacy behind because your children took part in your transformation and realized that they can help other people do the same.

Maybe that is the greatest legacy you can give your children, to let them participate in your transformation and learn life skills that are priceless. Maybe you why is to plant strong enough seeds in their garden so they will keep on harvesting the fruits long after you are gone. If your why is strong enough, then the hard work will actually not feel like hard work at all.

Have You Found Your WHY Yet?

Are you doing anything for your children today that feels like a sacrifice? Are you working at a job that you don't like that much and tell yourself that you are doing it for your kids or some other lame excuse? If so, how's that working out for you? Do you realize that you are actually leading by example in everything you do? Which are you demonstrating, a struggle or that you are thriving, with that decision of staying where you feel stuck?

When you are working on your transformation towards your goals and dreams and getting your children involved you are leading by example of thriving, from day one, even if it does not feel that way right away.

Are you ready to find you true why and do what you love and reap the benefits you deserve in your life? The state of thriving is an energetic state which happens instantaneously when you decide to live your life in the state of thriving attitude. What's stopping you from making that decision?

How Do You Feel When You Think About Your WHY?

Is your why, your children? If so, then how can you motivate yourself to do the rituals, the exercises and the work needed to succeed? Make the decision right now, to transform your life. Make the decision to take charge and follow the rituals and methods given to you by people who have already used them to succeed.

All the methods in this book work. The methods are actual footprints of success made by successful people. Have you ever walked in heavy snow before? Do you make new tracks or do you walk in the path that successful people already made in the snow? I have a lot of experience in walking in snow and although making new tracks is fun, it is very hard if you are walking all day. Life is a marathon, not a sprint.

I choose to walk in the footprints any day. Have you ever seen migrating birds fly? They use the momentum of one another to make the flight easier; why not use the momentum that has already been created in the world by successful people and make the transformation that much easier for you?

Can You Name Your Why Right Now?

Can you come up with a strong why right now? Can you and perhaps even your children work towards something together, a common why? The answer is yes, you can if you want to!

Now it is time for you to tell yourself why you want to transform your life and take action. You could find a charity or a cause that you are interested in and use it to fuel your success story.

Remember that financial goals are just one type of a goal. You could have a goal to be the greatest role model in your children's life, or be the biggest donation contributor in your church, city or even country. There are no limits on how many goals you set. What type of person do you need to be today to become what you have in mind?

Can you take action today toward becoming that person, what can you do now? Can you teach someone what you are doing? Can you do some volunteer work in the community, can you spend time teaching others what you already know?

Could you set up a group that meets every week to strive towards a common goal for the neighborhood for example? There are no limit on what your why should be and will be. Do you want to change the world, if so, why?

How does it make you feel when you think about it? The how is not so important now, the why is the most important part, because when you are driven by a strong why that makes you feel great and you are constantly thinking about the results with a great feeling, the how will reveal itself on your path.

My why, is to inspire 5 million people in the next 5 years to want to grow and learn, find their why and start their transformation. My why, is to help people learn how to be happier, smile more and how to feel better. My why is to save lives.

I am already changing lives, saving lives and transforming lives, I am truly living in alignment with my why, just the fact that you are reading this book right now is a big part of my why. Thank you and I mean that from the bottom of my heart!

Summary

- Finding your why, gives you a reason big enough to persist in your journey to succeed.

- When you have found your why and if your why is strong enough, no-one can stop you, not even you.

11. Great Manager

Great Manager

To becoming a really great manager can be done by simple common sense but having common sense is not as common as we might assume.

The big problem when you start to become a manager that manages a team, is that you do not really think about management matters because you do not know them. Things normally go wrong because you have never really thought about it and your lack of experience did not expect it. Management is about taking timeout to ask yourself the correct questions so that you can answer the questions yourself with your own common sense.

When you get more managerial responsibility, your first option is the easy option. Do exactly what is expected of you. You are new to this position so people will understand. You can learn from your mistakes and even better, from the mistakes of others as well. Those extra little problems are just common sense, so try to deal with them when they pop up. Grow into your position slowly and surely.

Option two, is far more exciting. Turn yourself in to a mega manager.

Once you become a manager, you gain control over your own work. Not all of it, but some of it. You can change things as it pleases you.

You can do things in a different ways. You actually have the power to make a huge impact. You can shape your surroundings and the company even with your methods, you will impact the and control your own work atmosphere.

In a bigger company, your options may be restricted by the existing corporate culture. You could do like the crab. Make changes sideways. Don't fight with an existing corporate system. Your job is to work better within the already existing culture or system. In a smaller business, the impact that you and your team has upon the culture are much deeper and your options are probably more versatile there. Your impact on the company's success is respectively much greater.

So once you start working more efficiently, this will be quickly noticed and recognized. Nothing gets more attention and faster approvals than great success.

Wherever you work, don't be surprised by the shock your colleagues will show when you first get serious about becoming a mega manager.

The thought of starting alone, may be intimidating to you, you may not see yourself as a David against the Goliath.

You can count on resistance showing up when you start to change things. Your hope lies in convincing your team that what you are doing, can only do them good. You also need to convince everyone else that these changes are not going to do them any harm. The good news are that soon others might follow you lead.

One example is when a firm from Iceland called Solbright Ltd wanted to be introduced to South Korean methods (Hyundai's to be precise) into their structure. They sent a small team to South Korea to learn the methods there.

On their return, they were ridiculed by their coworkers, who saw them as management pawns.

So instead they formed their own team and were send off to work in a different corner of the plant where they applied their new knowledge in isolation.

Slowly, but surely, their example spread through the factory and positive changes followed.

Faces of a Manager

The manger of a small team has a few major roles to play

Being a Planner

A Manager has to have great long term vision. The higher you climb, the further you will have to be able to project your vision into the future.

While a team member will be working towards known goals, a manager must look further into the future to see and make sure that these goals are selected intelligently.

By having the vision all the way towards the goal and using that vision to identify the final significances of different plans, the manager will then select the ideal plan for the team and implement it.

By taking into an account the needs of future projects, the manager ensures that work is not repeated over and over again nor that problems are tackled too late in the process. The manager will take appropriate action to ensure that all the necessary resources are assigned and arranged as well.

Being a Provider

A manager has the information and knowledge about the materials which the team needs. The manager often possessed the power of influence to acquire things which no one else in the team could.

A manager is important because no one else can do that part. There are some rights which the manager holds exclusively within the team, and the manager must exercise this to help the team to work and move forward.

Being a Protector

The team needs to be protected against any uncalled for accusations or being told off by a less free thinking manager. In any company, there are short-term excitements which can lead the staff off track from the important issues. A manager should be there to protect them against these situations and keep his team on track.

When a new project comes up for your team, you are responsible for costing it, in terms of time, so that your team is given a manageable deadline.

If any person on your team brings forward a good idea, you must make sure it receives a fair hearing and that your team knows and understands the outcome of that hearing. If someone on your team has any problems with the company, you have to deal with it right away.

That was a slightly formal approach. If you don't like formal then here is a different approach, a manager could provide:

Ways of Communication:

Use Text

Words are necessary to communicate without misunderstanding but words alone will not make your clients excited enough to buy your product.

Use Tones

The use of your voice will show different things based on how your tone is being used. You can display anger, enthusiasm, fear, contempt and much more just with your tone of voice. Make sure you know how to use this amazing tool effectively.

Body language

How do you use your eyes, your face expressing, your hands and your complete body and how do you recognize a staff member or a client's body language.

What do you do when you get irritated and loose interest? Do you tap your fingers, rub your forehead? What about when you are impatient, do you tap your fingers, play with a pencil or with your keys maybe? Learning how to recognize, translate and understand the body language of your staff members or client's sets you several steps ahead.

The perfect way to communicate is to use all of the above! A great manager will give a lot of examples how to communicate correctly to show the big difference and the importance of right and wrong. Good managers let their staff practice as much as possible to understand the game of body language. Your energy speaks way before you say anything, remember that.

Vision

One of the most mentioned features of great managers is that of outstanding vision.

The meaning of vision which concerns you as a manager is the ability to see a clear image of what the future should be like or will be like. This has nothing to do with prediction but everything to do with optimism. It is a focus for the whole team's motion, which provides continuous lasting drive and which bring and keeps your team together.

A great vision has to be something that connects your team with you in common purpose. This implies two things:

- You need to decide where you and your team are headed.

- You have to communicate this vision and make them fully understand it.

Communicating a vision is not just a case of painting it in large bold letters from corner to corner in your office wall, but instead is about bringing the entire team together to recognize your vision and to begin to share it with you.

A valuable vision must become a tool for guidance for the decisions and actions you and your team make.

This vision can be hard to pin down and hard to define usefully. A vision may even be unworkable.

So there is an extra phase which assists in its communication. Ones you have identified your vision, you can bring it to life and demonstrate it with a solid goal. This leads to the creation of the a mission statement. Let's first consider what a mission is, and then return to the vision.

A mission has two important qualities:

- it should be strong, but achievable given sufficient effort and time.

- it must be easy to tell when it has been accomplished.

To maintain positive ongoing motivation, the implementation of the vision might also have a time limit so that people can speed up their activity rather than getting winded in the initial momentum.

The size of your vision depends upon how high you have climbed up the management ladder in your organization and so does the time limit that you set yourself for each project based on the mission statement in the organization.

Top managers in multinational corporations look further into the future than the project leader in divisional recruitment. The top managers may be looking at a strategy for the next thirty years, while project leaders may be concerned with attracting the current cream of the crop from the graduation seniors this year for employment in the next two or three years.

A new manager will want a mission which can be achieved within a few years.

If you become trapped on a mission, think about using quality as your focus since it is something you can build on. Once you have established a few possible mission statements, you can communicate your vision and make decisions accordingly.

Your vision should be with no time limit and inspiring. It is the driving force, that continues even after accomplishing the mission statement.

Walt Disney's vision was to make people happy, and that is exactly what he did.

Your vision might be something, with less focus on the customer but instead more on you team, like making their job interesting and fulfilling.

There is no need to place you vision statement on the information board. Doing so could result in laughter and contempt. If your vision is not communicated to your team by what you say, visualize and do things, then you're not applying it yourself. Your vision is a tool for you to motivate yourself and once you have realized what you vision really is, act on it in every decision you make now and in the future.

Prescience

Prescience is something you really have to work at, having the intelligence of the future. As a protector, you need to know ahead of time the external events which might impact your team. Knowledge is the key:

- Information you hear.
- Information you gather.
- Information you infer.

Good information is vital. Studies of decision making in companies shows that the fast and critical decisions are normally not due to intuitive and/or amazing leadership but rather from an established information method covering relevant information in regards to that decision. Managers who have access to all the information that is relevant in each case, can quickly make an educated decision.

The effects upon you and your team often originate from inside the company and this is where you must establish keen interest.

If you don't keep your eyes open you are not ready to protect your team. If your manager comes back from an important meeting, sit down with him or her right after the meeting and have a talk.

There is no need to interrogate employees, merely ask the right questions. If there are answers, then great and you hear them and note them down. If there are none, you know to explore somewhere else.

By providing the manager with good helpful ideas, you will benefit from their gratitude and future confidence in you.

Get information from other divisions of the company as well and don't forget the secretaries and receptionists. They are often the first to know everything.

Some people love this part of the job, it makes them feel like real politicians or a Russian agent in a James Bond film. Others just hate it, for exactly the same reasons.

This must be done or you will be unprepared, but don't let it become a fixation.

Gathering detailed information is not enough, you have to do something with it. Try to predict the next logical step from any changes you see within and externally as well.

This can become complex, try to restrict yourself to guessing only one step. When sales numbers show a tailing off for the current product, then the development department might be expected to be pressured for tighter schedules; if you are in publicity, then there may soon be a request for launch material, if you are in sales, you might be asked to establish potential demand and practical pricing levels, you get it! Prepare but keep your guessing to only one step.

Now that you know this, you can have all the relevant information ready for when it is requested, and you and your team will shine.

Flexibility

One of the main challenges is to avoid the perfect answer to daily questions. There are few things as boring for you and your team, as pulling out the same universal perfect answer to every situation. It is also incorrect. Each situation, and each person, are unique and no perfect answer will apply that uniqueness.

There is one exception. You are the manager, so review each situation with a fresh eye, and create the answer.

Your knowledge and experience is your best tool in exploring the problem and in evolving your responses.

If the conventional response could work, you might still try something new.

By trying variations upon the common models, you evolve new and potentially better models.

If they don't work, you do not need to keep on repeating them but if they do work, then you have adapted and evolved. Great job!

Purposeful flexibility is not just a predefined exercise to find the best answer. The situation and the environment are continually changing and the rate of change is generally increases side be side along with advancing technology.

If you don't frequently adapt to lodge these changes, then the solution will become obsolete before you know it and no longer be suitable.

By not being on your toes and being adaptable could easily cause sluggishness and inactivity. By not adapting, the excitement of your team becomes absent as well as fresh new ideas become lost.

Stimulate your team with changes of focus. This includes efforts for detailed quality improvements, mission reports, team building activities, delegated authority, and much more. How often are you going to bring this up with new issues? That's up to you.

Trying to focus on too many subjects can distract or prevent the accomplishments. On the other hand, shifts in focus will keep your team sharp and keep them excited.

Leading by example, by adapting this viewpoint, you will also stimulate fresh ideas from your own team because they see that it is a normal part of the team practice to adopt and experiment with innovation.

Plan, Monitor, Review

Before you start anything, you must stop and think before you act. What is the objective? How can it be achieved? What are the option?, Who needs to be included? What will it cost? Is it worth it?

When you have a solid plan, stop and think about how to ensure that your plan is functioning properly. You must find ways of monitoring your progress, even if it is just setting deadlines for smaller milestones, checking the customer replies or tracking the number of outdated products which have to be discarded. Select something which shows progress and start that process to ensure it will take place.

Set a date on which where you will stop and go over your plan with the data you gathered from the observation.

If you have something to do then firstly consider the technique, then the assignment.

In a meeting where you are going to decide which steps to take for the new company campaign, start by paying no attention to anything to do with the campaign it self, but instead decide:

- how the meeting should be held,

- who can normally contribute,

- how your team can generate good ideas,

- what criteria is involved in the decisions,

- if there is a more efficient or effective way of achieving those results.

If you resolve these topics first, all will be achieved far more easily.

There is no magic formula, there are no correct answers nor wrong answers to these questions. The point is that they need to have an answer to each one, so that the task will be completed professionally.

What defines a great coach is similar to what defines a great manager, it is the way you ask questions and bring out the right answers form your team. You make ordinary workers extraordinary by the questions you ask. All solutions are available already and through common sense and smart thinking, your questions bring them out.

Once the questions are modeled, you can be creative on how to move forward with the campaign. Also, ask everybody in the company to contribute an idea to the campaign as well, you never know when you stumble upon the diamond in the rough.

This takes a few minutes and an office assistant to organize, it provides a quick thrill of excitement throughout the company. It sharpens everyone's mind on the new campaign and all the staff feel some ownership in the campaign. You start the meeting with many new ideas which you use to select a person to get a bonus or an employee of the month award.

In a perfect world all managers are very smart, information is precise and always presented. In this world it would be possible for you to sit down and to plan the strategy for your group.

Unfortunately, in the real world, managers are individuals, information is rarely complete and continuously inaccurate and the unexpected always arrives awkwardly.

The situation is never just black and white, but always presented in shades of gray.

Your planning is only as good as your best guess in the present situation. The review is when you understand the results and assume that success is emerging from the plan.

The review is not just to fine-tune your plan but also to evaluate the test and to incorporate the new, useful information which you have collected and merging it into the creation of the next logical step forward. Now you should be ready for essential changes.

Body Language!

While giving your message to your staff watch their body language very closely. It tells you so much more than the words that will come out of their mouths. This is something every person reveals without knowing it.

Arms crossed means a closed mind, hard to get the message in. Break the ice first, get him or her to open up for conversation!

Ticking fingers or pen is impatience. Get to the point, you are probable talking around the main subject! What do you want?

Rubbing chin when the person is very interested, you got his or her attention, now hold it and get what you want!

Rubbing the forehead and not understanding. Being tired and irritated maybe so be careful here!

Get to the point but first step back. Make a joke or whatever is interesting for him or her and then get them back into the conversation!

The cattle position means that they are very interested.

He or she is 100% agreeing with you and interested. These are just a few out of hundreds of kinds of body language there is out there to read, just for you. New book mainly focused on body languages is on the task list, so stay tuned.

12. The Pipeline

Pipelines to Success

This is not a typical theoretical chapter you read in a book, this chapter is more of a blueprint than anything else. How to actually do the things that can make you millions in the long run. Yes, once again you hear me saying it, it's a marathon not a sprint. You can start doing many small things that will add up and become great success after a while. Please understand before reading on, that if you want to be successful, it is going to take a lot of effort and time, regardless of how talented you are. Remember this as well, hard work will outperform talent any day. Most people overestimate what they can accomplish short term, while they massively underestimate what they can accomplish long term, for example in one decade or so.

All the information you are about to read are based on the year 2017, when this is written, so if you are reading this later than 2017, then some names, companies or services might have changed. The blueprint will nevertheless stay the same regardless of what the company or service is called at the time you read this.

Now we are going to cover a few things you can do today and start earning money in as little as one day from now and if you put your back into it, stay persistent and keep going, then in about one to five years from now you will be making a whole lot of money with any of these methods I am going to teach you here. We will cover methods on how to make money with video content, by creating music regardless weather you have music talent or not, writing books and by doing seminars online. These steps are written for beginners that have not done any of these steps before. If you have, then you might pick up a few tricks to add on to your arsenal by reading this.

Video Content

You see more and more video content all over the internet today. Therefore we are overloaded with information. We can watch and see whatever we like, whenever we like. So how can you make money by delivering video content? There are several ways of doing that, but I would ask myself right now if you are thinking about getting into video content to make money, what you are good at?

When is you energy at its best, what do you enjoy more than anything and never get tired of learning about or discussing? These are simple questions for you to answer and then you can take the next step. You could be really good a criticizing for example.

Criticizing movies. Gossiping, telling jokes, talking about the news and discussion another point of view. Great at improvising meals, presenting them and cooking. You might be really good at finding something wrong with things in general. You might be great at finding and using coupon. The point is, that whatever that thing is that you are great at, it does not matter, because there is an audience out there waiting for you to start delivering value.

Before we start exploring your options and going into all the practical things, I must warn you. If you are not willing to give this at least one year before expecting any residual income through video content sharing, then I suggest you move on to the next chapter, then this is not for you.

Do not get your hopes up and expect to become the next one hit wonder with one video and getting 100 million views in the first week, it simply does not work that way.

Now on the other hand if it will happen, then it will be a very pleasant surprise for you, a bonus. Once you have the topic you are going to cover and share, then you need to commit to yourself to create one video per day or one video per week for the next 365 days. The difference between one each day and one each week is the type of presentation you are giving in the videos.

Straightforward almost non editing videos that have the duration of 1-3 minutes are daily videos, but if you have a show or scheduled events weekly, then you will most likely spent 1-2 days preparing it and 1-2 days editing and finalizing it. Now you must understand that these numbers are not set in stone, this varies quite a bit, but these are very likely numbers for you to go by, to start with.

Now that you have selected your topic, you are further ahead than most.

You will need a camera and yes you can use your phone's video camera, they are pretty decent today, some are even very good HD cameras. You will most likely need some kind of microphone if you are interviewing others or talking straight into the camera "to the audience".

If you are sharing content like cooking for example, it does not matter as much whether you have a good microphone or not. If you are demonstrating something that you do in the videos, creating, baking, building or something of that nature and it does not require good clear sound recording then there is no need for an external microphone, the one in the phone will do just fine.

Lighting is very important if you intend to film indoors, but outdoors it's not as important. If you are a beginner in film making then you can find tutorials online for anything you want to do. You can find software that is completely free to use to edit your videos, just search online for them.

The most important thing I can tell you right now is that you will probably suck at first, but that's OK. We, the audience, want to be able to see you grow, that makes you even more personal and human through the lens. You want to get your videos done and keep posting them. If you have a delusions about getting them perfectly done, then you might as well just go ahead and skip this chapter. Perfect means never! Done is the new perfect!

This is the setup you are going to follow, you are going to provide free value to people, you are going to educate or entertain people with whatever it is that you are great at. About one year from now, then you can start to create merchandise, sell ads, product placements and so forth based on your topics and how popular your will become by then. The first year is about getting audiences and building a community. Don't worry you will make money the whole time, just not a lot to start with.

If you want to start with a very basic simple way of starting your company or brand, this is a straightforward approach that you can follow.

Start by getting a Google email (assuming that Google will be still around when you read this). Then sign up for their AdSense service or similar ad revenue service if that service has changed by the time you read this.

This service will allow you to identity yourself through your Google account and connect your bank account to your AdSense account. Now you are set, you are ready to start monetizing your videos. Next you need to create a YouTube channel with your Google email and once you have set it up, then you can go into your settings for that channel and connect your AdSense account to your YouTube account.

A side note here, if you know any person that has a lot of views and is not monetizing their videos, you can connect your AdSense account to their YouTube channel, but to do this you will need their approval of course and you might be asked to teach them to create their own advertising account when you ask for this, but it does not hurt to ask if you know someone who is not making the most of all the views he or she is getting and does not care whether you seize the moment and reap the benefits.

This way you can start making some money right away.

Now that you have setup your YouTube channel and connected it to your AdSense account you are ready to upload your first video. The type of ads you can display on each video when this is written are, display ads (desktop only), overlay ads, sponsored cards and skippable video ads.

I would recommend to keep them all on and let Google work their magic because their artificial intelligence in marketing is pretty impressive. Now you can film your short 1-3 minute video each day. One video per day is for B players and if you are an A player, like I suspect you are, then you will do 1-3 videos per day and upload them all.

How are people finding you videos online, you might be wondering?

The more platforms you can share your videos across and cross reference it, the more visible your video will be. Make a title that is very descriptive of the content and if you have a brand name include it in the title if you want, but that's up to you.

Next you need to describe the video as well as possible so that the automatic search engines pick up the right words from your description when someone is looking for that particular topic.

Then you need to select a few keywords, these words will have to be in your long description of the video to work the best for optimizing the search on the video online.

You can find software that will help you in creating the best keywords for the best exposure, just look around for one, you might even find a browser add-on that will do it for you. I use an add-on service called vidIQ for example.

Once you have everything ready and you have uploaded the video, then you need to share the video in as many platforms as possible. An example of a description of a video you upload could be something like this:

I shot this video in front of the library last night in "your town" and I noticed that the roof was about to come off. So I threw a stone at the roof and guess what happened. Then list all your channels and get the connections to cross reference the materials between social media platforms. See examples for links, keywords and description for your videos, here on the sample page.

http://OurRoadwithoutBoundaries.com/links

You list all your connections in the description, Pinterest, Twitter, Google+, Tumblr, Instagram, Facebook and so forth.

Don't forget to put your YouTube URL there as well, because when you share this on your other platforms you will use the description as the status for the share on each platform. You will link it all together this way.

Once you start to share your videos you need a hashtag for your brand as well, example #yourbrand #yourtopic #yourname, this would be a great start. The more you can link everything together the more visible you will become.

You will need to take some time each week to share your videos with groups or people that are discussing similar topics. You will need to follow people with similar interests and you need to be active in liking pictures and videos you find online that match your interests area or your niche.

If you want to add extra value to your videos and create subtitle for your audience, then you can find a free software online called subtitle workshop, which I personally use myself, you can see an example of a subtitle on the sample page.

http://OurRoadwithoutBoundaries.com/links

It is a very simple program to create subtitle that you can add to your videos and you will save them as .srt files, YouTube accepts .srt files and then your audience can watch your video with subtitles. This also gives you the opportunity to share your .srt file with a person who speaks another language and you can get it translated and upload it as well, then you can broaden your audience even more, providing subtitles in multiple languages.

You will see good results in as little as 12 months from the day you start, today probably, because only people who are serious about their career and wealth would pick up this book and I know you are an A player.

You have to be persistent, to be able to succeed. I promise you that if you stick to it, then you will be rewarded handsomely. There will be endless possibilities once you have a brand recognition. People will seek you out to throw money at you. Remember how we discussed visualizing and writing your future into existence in the earlier chapters, if you don't remember, then go back now and read them, because you need to write your story right before it unfolds and keep doing that throughout the process of becoming a world known brand. If you do remember reading it earlier in the book, then you know how important it is for you to keep yourself on track and manifest this desired future with your mindset and with the action you take at the same time every day.

Here is a very simple but powerful exercise for you to execute and connect more with your audience if you are doing any videos where you talk into the camera (to your followers). Stair at the mirror about one foot (30 cm) away from the mirror and choose only one eye, either the right or the left.

Stair into your eyeball on the eye you have selected. You only need to do this exercise one time for it to make a huge difference in the level of power you present your materials to your audience. Stair into the eyeball for 5 minutes and while you do so feel free to laugh, cry or whatever feelings break out. You can even practice talking to the eyeball.

Once you finish the 5 minutes of staring at one of your eyeballs, take the phone or camera, which ever you are using to film and look at the phone or camera lens. If you use a phone then find the camera and pretend that is your eyeball, if you are using a camera then use the middle of the lens as your eyeball.

Now close your eyes and think about what makes you the most happy in the world, it can be a past or future event or a person. Bring forth into your body a great feeling that comes with this thought and feel how your energy level lifts up and you get energized.

Once you feel it, then open your eyes, pick up the phone and press record and look straight into your eyeball (lens) and deliver your materials like you've never done before, with passion and more energy than ever. Your audience will feel your presence.

You will get better and better at this as you do more and more videos, but remember since you have this information now and do it right from day one, then you will be amazing very soon!

Creating Music Without Music Talent

Do you think it would be nice to receive a check in the mail each month for a lifetime from the Performance Rights Organizations or PROs (in the US that's BMI, ASCAP, and SESAC). They collect songwriting performance royalties from music users and then pay songwriters and rights holders (publishers) royalties for a lifetime. In Iceland we have something called STEF, which is the same unit as PROs.

"Hold on, I cannot create music!" I don't care if you can or not, do you want royalty checks for life or not?

I create music and receive checks each month and yet I don't play any instruments, I don't sing and I do not understand notes. Then how in the world do I create music?

Its super simple, I don't. I am going to take you step by step through the process of how I create music and become the lyrics and music writer without music talent. You are getting this information here in this book while I charge two thousand dollar to coach my clients and help them set up and build this money funnel.

Here you are on your own, but with your focus and enthusiasm you can build it on your own.

Of course you would get much more help with the coaching but my time is very valuable. At the same time I am confident that you can take this advice and implement it on your own. You are smart, I know you are, because you made it this far in the book. Let's get started building this money stream for a lifetime.

Before I start, think about it, have you ever heard a song on the radio before it was a hit and thought to yourself, "This will be a hit"? If you have, then you might make a lot more money with this pipeline than you can imagine. Now you are going to learn to build it here.

Step 1.

First thing is first, what genre music do you like? I like pop, techno and drop step music. Now you need to find a platform that suits you the best to find ideas. I use a website called Pond5 at the time of writing this book, there are several websites out there that provide similar services. You could even use YouTube to search for music that you like. I suggest searching for music in a genre you like and preferably an instrumental version, but you can use fully mastered tracks with vocals, but this will depend on the music talent you find and place in your pipeline. Let's not get ahead of ourselves here.

Once you find an instrumental song you really like, then save the location of that song and let's move on to step two.

Step 2.

Now you need to find a music talent to create the music for you that you can claim this song which we have not created yet, as your own. You have to find your preferred platform to do this. I use a website called Fiverr at the time of writing this.

You want to browse through the talent available on the platform you choose, again there are many places that offer similar services for talented people all over the globe. A place where contractors can offer their services. Even if these guys have super talent, they don't have the vision you have, you are going to create magic, you just don't know it yet.

I am going to tell you how I created my pipeline and I suggest you do the same. You will narrow it down to about 5-7 artist, by listening to their demos and getting the feel for their creative abilities.

The more you listen to demos the more opinionated you will become of whom you want to work with. Now that you have narrowed this down to 7 artist, you will send them all an offer on the music creation, your gig or task, whatever you want to call this process. I will refer to it from now on as a gig, as it is what the website I use, Fiverr, calls it. You will send them all the same letter and it could be something like this:

"Hi my name is Huni and I am looking for an artist to create music for my projects. I need full rights for the music creation, here is a link to a song that I really like.

Can you create an a similar instrumental track, around 3 minutes long and how much would it cost for you to create this instrumental track, with enough differences to not break any copyright music laws?"

I paid anywhere from $10 to $50 for the creation of each track in the beginning stages, when I was searching for the artist I wanted to work with. You will get 7 different versions of the same song, each artist will put their own fingerprint on it. Listen to them all at the same time. I mean, wait for the delivery from all 7 artist before you listen. Now listen to them all back to back and then again the next day.

Select the artist with your gut, what do you like the most, who seemed very straight forward while communicating with you and so forth. Look at all the aspects of dealing with that artist. Great, now you have completed step 2, congrats! You have your music artist. Your have found your first link in the pipeline.

Step 3.

The topic of the song. This is the fun part. I will demonstrate two different methods here.

First method is to try and create a little by playing the song over and over and mumble some word out loud until they sound OK and the second method is to write a list of sentences and pass it on to the lyrics artist you will find.

In method one I create at least the beginning and one chorus to steer the song in the right direction. In this song called Time which is the first song I created to claim royalties from as the song and lyrics writer. I knew I wanted to create a song for my brand Watchon Indicator.

The main character can travel through time and the main focus of this brand is teaching children to learn from others, not having to make their own mistakes all the time. A smart human learns for his mistakes but a brilliant human learns from the mistakes of others.

Here is the exact copy of the message I sent to my lyrics artist, before she was in my pipeline:

"Hi are you interested to help me with lyrics to a children song? I have plenty of work if you are interested and if I like your work.

Send me a line if you are interested, this is my next project to put lyrics to and here is Watchon's homepage http://watchon.club this is the brand I am working on.

This is a sample of the 3 minute long song I am working on right now.

Look forward hearing from you.

Sincerely, Huni."

I sent this message to 5 artists to find the one I wanted to work with, the same applies to you. You need to get a few done to find the person that will create what you like.

Find the best match to your needs. Next, using method one, I did put together these few lines with time reference points in the instrumental song I had already created, or should I say had my music artist create for me.

The next step was to send the artist my instrumental song and partial lyrics and explain what I wanted to accomplish.

Here are the very first lines I created, please remember I don't know music, but just did this anyway, that should be your attitude as well because the talent you are recruiting will pick you up and create magic for you. That is how I feel each time I create with my pipeline. I feel like I am actually working with magicians. Here is the first lines:

"00:14 Hey, how are you today?

00.18 Are you ready to come and play?

00:22 Were going on a journey together to learn from others just like our mothers

00:29 let's get ready to start the ride buckle up and do it right now you are ready to get started

1.2.3 now lets go go

00:43 Hey, hey, hey, you are O, OK, let's go travel together! Let's go see what's in history. Let's go see it together!

Now we can use the time, we can use the time, we can use the time to learn.

We can use the time, we can use the time, we can use the time and learn to do it right"

The artist then sends back something which you go ever and send back, there will be something that you will not like, most likely, in the first run, I am pretty sure of it. It is your creation, don't cut corners. Make sure it's right, not perfect but right. Remember, done is the new perfect! This might go back and forth for a while, until you feel it's right, then if you have selected your lyrics artist well, you can ask for a demo from the artist. Your lyrics artist will sing the lyrics over the instrumental song, this can be done with a phone recording, this is only for timing references once you take the song to the next step and send it to a singer.

Before we go to step 4, I will demonstrate method 2 here. The second song I did, I simply created a list of sentences which I sent to the lyrics artist and said what I wanted to accomplish. I wanted to create a song about how you manifest your dreams into your reality, so I sent this list to the lyrics artist:

"What you believe is what you get. It's already done. You become who you need to be now.

How will you be when you have everything you want? How will you talk? How will you walk?

How will you speak? Become that person right now. Step into that identity now.

To attract a perfect partner you first have to become the perfect partner. It's done!

Believe you will and find your WHY. Your HOW will be revealed to you if you know it will be so.

Act like it's already done. Visualize, feel, smell, taste and experience it like it's already true.

What you think about most of the time with the most emotion behind it is what you get.

Can you imagine how great it will feel?

Can you enjoy the journey? Enjoy the journey

Live with passion Failure is one step closer to success

Success is created first in your mind. What you think is what you get the power of the mind is unlimited

Love yourself unconditionally so others can as well. You are love. Your message is strong and powerful, do you know what it is?

Fear is only a trigger of emotions based on your beliefs. Change your beliefs and conquer your fears. Shift your mind to manifest your dream.

Paint your dream into existence on your canvas of reality. Dream big, fail fast, take action and see what you created."

These are two totally different methods of working through the process. One, sing it and the other, write it. Then step back and let the magicians take over to create the magic.

Step 4.

Now you have your instrumental music, lyrics and demo which the singer will use as reference. Now you have probably guessed it already. You go to the platform of your choice and find 4-5 singers you want to sing on the track for you. Once you find your 5 singers, you make an offer on all 5 of them and write to them that you need commercial, full rights to the vocals. This was about $50 per song for me at the time to find the one I wanted to work with.

Once you have your singer make sure that you get high quality files with clean vocals only and no background sounds at all, so you need to find a singer that has access to a studio or has his/her own semi-pro setup. Now you have the song, lyrics and vocals, well done!

Step 5.

Now the same process will repeat itself in this step, maybe if you are lucky your music talent you hired, he might be able to mix and master the track for you, if not you need to find one, using the same method. Find a music mixer and master talent for your final stage of production in the pipeline. You can use these words to search for one on you preferred contractor platform "I will mix and professionally master your track". Once you find your mix master, you have a final product, congrats! Your first song you own the rights to completely. Well done!

You are not done yet, now you have to claim the rights to this creation so you can get paid for the rest of your life.

Step 6.

Register your song with whomever does that in your country, in my country, Iceland, we have something called STEF, where I register my music. Once you have that done, you will have an identification number to your track. Here is an example of the registration number for one of my songs Time, ISRC: IS-V44-16-34201.

Once you have this completed you are ready to send the track to radio stations and wherever they play your type of music genre.

I offer my music on iTunes, Google Play, Amazon and Spotify. In the beginning I needed to decide if I wanted to do it directly by myself or use a music aggregator and after some research I decide to let the professionals handle this as well, because I simply don't have the time to learn all that.

I went with a service called Catapult and they provide me with registration in the US market and as well the rest of the world.

They also provide me with something called YouTube sound collection service, which is an algorithm that looks for you song on YouTube and if it finds it on any videos there, then they automatically claim it for you and you get royalties from the ads on that video, regardless of whose channel it is on.

Now you have all the steps needed to create your pipeline of music creation, no music talent needed.

I did many mistakes before creating the final pipeline and if you look at the YouTube channel for the Watchon Indicator brand you can tell there are several songs there which I cannot claim royalties from since I did it the wrong way. Don't worry about how to do this wrong, you have the correct method here and you can follow it and start building your multiple income streams as soon as you want it, as soon as you are ready.

You probably guessed it already, the most expensive part of the process is setting up the pipeline in the beginning, paying five to seven artist each step of the way, but once you have it done, if you did it the right way like I have, then you can create a new song for a total price of $100-$400 each time, depending on your artists and whether or not you are going to create a music video to the song. That will cost you money.

Marketing your songs is a very important part for you to get noticed. I suggest using the aggregators and I would not worry about starting to market anything until after 6 months when you have at least 6 songs in your portfolio. Check out these two examples, which I demonstrated here to see how they turned out.

http://OurRoadwithoutBoundaries.com/links

Write and Self-Publish Your Books

Why not write and learn to become one of the talked about authors in the world. Do you like explaining to people how something works or do you like to tell stories? Maybe your story is something you could share with the world, is it worth writing about?

First off let me tell you on this path you will create 2-4 books per year, for the next 5 years. Sounds like a lot, I know, but I want to remind you that this is not a sprint, this is a marathon. Why not start with a book around 10.000 words. Easy target.

You pick your topic and start writing. You can start by selecting your topic and then imagine how many chapters the book will have, create a basic skeleton for the book. At first you don't even have to name the chapters unless you have a very good idea about where you story is heading. If you choose to write your story for example, then you can divide the chapters into phases. The beginning, learning, the problem and the redemption.

Once you start to write it, then the chapters can be broken into smaller sections. This is a very simple example of course. Let's say that you want to write a children's book.

Who will be reading it, children that can read or parents? Are they going to interact with the child in a way that the child has to respond to the reading? Are you going to ask questions to the reader or simply tell a story?

Is the story going to teach them values or do you want to write something that has pure entertainment value? Regardless of whether you think you can write or not, let me assure you that does not matter, the only thing that you have to have in mind is that the worse you are off in grammar and structure and word use, the more expensive it will be to get the book edited, if you are looking for perfect. Done is the new perfect, remember that.

Here is a secret for you, you can have you book spell checked with automatic corrections on a computer. You can get people to spell check the book for you after you publish it, yes you read this correctly and you have probably seen some spelling errors in this book, well done, could you send it to me please, so I can update this book? I have personally published my books and then corrected then later, just like this one.

Example, when I published The Mentorian or Læringinn like the name is in Icelandic, after the first few people read the fantasy fairy tale, I got back corrections and suggestions, with over 40 spelling errors, so I simply double checked them and then uploaded a new file for the book.

That's the beauty of self-publishing and print-on-demand. You don't have hundreds or even thousands of book out there with spelling and grammatical errors. Print-on-demand is a service that will enable you to start selling your paperback copy of your book without printing a single copy.

The customer's order the books, the company then prints the book and ships it to the customer. This means that the next customer that bought my book, The Mentorian, in Icelandic (Læringinn) got it corrected when he received his printed copy of the book.

Those who bought it as an e-book, got theirs automatically updated. Back to you and your future in writing books and publishing them.

A question to ask yourself, how much time can you devote to writing?

If you are retired or like me at the time when I started writing, have a job where you can write during work hours you should be able to set yourself the goal to write about 1.000 words per day or 5-8 hours per day.

So you first book should be done after 10 days. If on the other hand you have a full-time job that does not allow you to do any writing during the day and you can only devote about three hours per day to writing, then there are some simple rules to follow to make sure you get the job done, turn off all distractions once you start to write, cell phone, emails, social media platforms and other distractions.

Use one hour before your work starts in the morning to write and 2 hours after work to write and you should be able to get at least 500 words per day. It's OK if you do more, this will only be your minimum word count per day to keep you on track.

You should be able to finish your first 10.000 word book in 20 days.

If you ever get a writer's block, just keep on writing about how hard it is to write and why you have the block. How it feels and so forth because then that will be one of the books you will publish in the first or second year of writing, how to overcome writer's blocks and why they occur and so forth. Yes you are getting it, I know you are. Now you start to see the opportunities in everything you do.

Your mind is working more efficiently now and you notice that whatever happens, it is monetizable. Now 20 days later you have your first short book ready that needs editing.

You can do several things now at this stage. You can go to websites like Fiverr or similar service sites where you can search for contractors to edit your book. My first editor was Ruth Coetzee, if you look her up just tell you she was recommended by Huni.

These will be very different quality editors of course, so I suggest finding 2-3 editors to edit your first book, to learn how they work and what you are looking for in a good editor. You might find one right of the bat, but very likely you will have to go through a few before you find someone that is good, that suits you.

Now at this stage you have a book ready to be published. Yes, I know you are concerned that it's not perfect! But wait, done is the new perfect, so then it must be perfect already!

You are right it's probably not good, but very likely it's better that you think it is. This is your first book out of at least 20 books you will publish in the next 5 years, so don't worry, you will get better and better.

The more you write and publish the less editing you will need. At one point in time you will be noticed and then you can go to a few big publishers and present the results you have accomplished so far.

Then you can have them fight over who gets the right to publish your next book and that is when you will start to see some good money come in from your book sales and once you first best seller is out, then the sales of all your previous books will go up as well.

Now that you have your first book edited and ready to publish, you need a cover to your book.

This can be done for as little as $5 on sites like Fiverr or similar sites. All you need is the title, subtitle and author's name and you can find someone to make a nice book cover for you for very little money. When you publish your books you also need an ISBN numbers, which is like a fingerprint for the book.

You need a separate ISBN numbers for each type of book you publish. If you publish an e-book and on paperback, then you need two ISBN numbers for that one book (two formats).

In my country of origin the government supports writers and we get our ISBN numbers for free, but I don't know how it is in your country.

Find out how you can get an ISBN number, if you can't get it for free, then you can simply look for it online, there are plenty of sites who are more than willing to sell you ISBN numbers. Once you have your ISBN number you want to create a bar code for that ISBN number and place that on the cover as well. I would search online for an ISBN bar-code creator. There are several free sites who do that for you see example here.

http://OurRoadwithoutBoundaries.com/links

Use the bar-code and ask the person who is doing the cover design to place it on the cover as well and to send you a clean cover as well because you can use the clean version for your e-book (not the same ISBN number for that version of your book and no need to have it on the cover there). Now that you have your cover done, your ISBN bar-code and your editing done, you are ready to publish the book. Congrats!

In these last steps I recommend two services that I use.

I want you to note that there are more options available then these two. The steps on other sites or with services should be very similar.

I use a service called Lulu to publish my paperback printed books.

When you publish on Lulu you can have the books become automatically available on Amazon and Barnes & Nobles bookstores as well, which I think is a very nice add-on for you as a self-published author. You will get much less revenue through those services, but it will expand your reach a whole lot.

Firstly create an account and then select the type of book you want to print.

I will demonstrate the process of "The Mentorian" which is the first book of three in a trilogy fantasy fairytale series. The book is around 13.000 words, which could easily represent your first book pretty accurately. I selected a product line of premium paperback, perfect bound, size A5, interior color black & white, paper quality 60#, cover finish gloss and shipping origin global. Then I put into the field where they ask how many pages the book contains, I wrote 78 pages. After I put that information in the site automatically gives me the spine measurements for the cover.

For The Mentorain book the measurements looked like this, spine width: 0.176 inches, cover size: 12.09 x 8.513889 inches and spine begins at 5.958333 inches.

These measurements are great to have for the person who does your book cover or if you know how to adjust an image you can do this yourself. You can always put your page numbers in on lulu to get the measurements before you order the cover for your book and that way you will have the cover in the right measurements right of the bat.

Next step is to type the title of the book and select the distribution of the book. Then you upload the script, the actual content and I recommend using pdf while uploading for print and doc format for uploading e-book, that's my recommendation.

If you selected to print the book like I did in black and white, then you need to make sure all images in the book are gray scale for more consistency in printing. If you selected to print in full color, then the images should be cmyk full color. When you create you e-book version make sure all images have no wrap, meaning no text on either side of the image.

Selecting black and white inside of the book makes it much cheaper to print, when this is written the cost of 78 page A5 book costs around $2.80 to print one copy. I sell my books through Lulu, Amazon, Barnes & Nobles and more, and the difference in royalty differs a lot. On Lulu I will get around $17 net profit while on other platforms only about $7. The books listed price is $24.95 for the paperback version we just covered here.

The final stage of publishing this paperback version of your book is uploading the cover image. I recommend using a single image from the cover designer, with the bar-code on it and the Lulu site will inform you if the cover fits to their suggested measurements or not. Then you put your description and publisher, which is you until you have your own publishing agent or company.

You are done publishing your paperback version now. Now it's time to order your proof copy of the book. Congrats with your first published book, you are now a published author.

For the e-book version you will upload a word document to Amazon, not a pdf.

You start by opening an account with Amazon to publish your e-book, you will use the clean cover to upload as the cover and you will use a new ISBN number for this version of the book.

The process is pretty self-explanatory after going through the paperback publishing steps. You will get automatically assigned an ASIN number, which is like a fingerprint identification used by Amazon, which will be connected to your ISBN number.

For you to get an author's page at Amazon you have to create it at AuthorCentral and you have to select which books you want to display on your author's page, remember that they will not appear automatically. See example of author's page.

http://OurRoadwithoutBoundaries.com/links

Get your books registered in the global ISBN registry. I have to print and deliver 3 copies to the national book library of Iceland and give them copies of my books to keep and register into the ISBN world registry.

I cannot tell you the way you should register your work, maybe your government supports writers and has a similar free system like Iceland does, I know for that South Africa has a similar system allocating free ISBN numbers for writers at the time of writing this book, but this part is up to you to find out how you do it in your country.

Worst case scenario you find a service online which you pay to have you book registered globally in the ISBN book registry and I do think that Lulu provides this service for you if you choose to use it for a small fee.

Congratulations you have published your first book as paperback and e-book. Now share this book with your friends through social media and ask them to share your book on their platforms as well. Don't forget to ask people for reviews on your books, for they do get you noticed.

Online Seminars

Do you own your own website? Are you branded? If you have your own website, whether branded or not yet, I recommend setting up online courses on your site, but keep in mind that you will not have any traffic to the site until you become someone people notice, when you become branded.

When the time comes that people start to put you name into the Google machine and search for other awesome courses you provide, you want your site to pop up in the search so you can grab those already interested potential clients.

If you are branded then this section might just be a pleasant reminder of what you can do to increase your customer base. Let's jump right into it!

When this book is written Udemy is the largest online learning marketplace with over 15 million students and growing. There are students that want to learn what you have to teach on Udemy actively searching for courses like the one you are going to create.

When you create a course you are going to make two types, one for Udemy and one for you own website, they will be very similar but the one on your own site is going to have less rules to follow, for you as the creator.

For example on your site your course can promote your other courses or other services freely, while on Udemy there are strict rules about leading your customers (students) away from the platform, you could be banned from the site for breaking these rules. On your site you can up-sell the client something more and better at the end of the course.

Giving the fact that Udemy is providing you with all the tools you need for free, you should have no problem complying with a few rules.

On your site do what you like, as far as to lead the customers to your other paid online courses or affiliated programs you might be associated with.

There is one downside to Udemy's platform as I write this, if you have a course that involves working in periods, for example your course is a training program, that requires your clients (students) to learn a trade and then use it for 7 days, then moving on to learn the next valuable lesson on top of the first skill, stacking them, then you will most likely be disappointed like I was. Udemy does not offer any tools to set a timer once you finish a lesson that will trigger the next lesson to open up after the timer has ran down to zero.

Udemy has great tools and great teaching videos and trainers that actually go over each lesson of your courses manually and watch to see you follow their guidelines, you will get feedback on what you need to fix and so on. This is the perfect place to learn to create your online courses and the best part, it's all 100% free.

By now, you know that whatever you do, from now on, everything you do is monetizable.

This means that you should for example write down all the steps you go through making your first online course and then make your second online course about making an online course.

You are going to follow these easy steps. Select a topic and present it, if you know it by heart then great if not, then use Google and research it and get the bits you need to complete the course. Most of your courses on Udemy will be made up by mostly videos. Here your exercise from earlier in the chapter will come in handy, how to engage more with the audience (the mirror exercise).

There are several subject to think about when filming for your course, how's the lighting, where are you filming, how is the sound quality? When you record yourself talking into the camera and then when you listen to the recording, you will notice background sounds that you cannot hear while shooting the course, sounds like the computer fan, refrigerator, air conditioning and many other sounds you don't notice because your brain is very good at keeping it from you on daily basis, just to keep you sane.

These sounds will not be accepted on Udemy for example, therefore you will need to get yourself an audio software to take that noise out.

I recommend a free open source software called Audacity, which I use as well. Then just search online for free courses or tutorials on how to take the noise out using Audacity. There are online courses and tutorials about almost anything you wish to learn, which you have to take advantage off.

Now you will set your target, how many courses you are going to produce, now that you are ready to give this at least 12 months and see how much you will be making by that time.

Every two weeks you will publish a course online and you are going to make every other course free to use, they can be shorter, but it has to be of great value to the client, this is for branding purposes and the secret of the pros, the more you give the more you get, this way the world will get to know you.

Each month you will make one course that you will charge for and one that is absolutely free. These are the minimum requirements.

You can easily do this, with a full time job, you can take 3 hours per day and 10 hours over the weekend to create courses. This is a sacrifice you are willing to make if you want a better life, if you want recurring income for life. Check these samples out here.

http://OurRoadwithoutBoundaries.com/links

Preferably you should not have to do any work after publishing your course, unless you need to update some information or something of that nature or answer a student's request.

Start today to create a very simple course online, it may be as simple as how to cook something or how to open a bottle with a certain tool, how to create a course online, how to write a book, how to surprise people, how to read people, how to stretch your body, how to monitor your diet or change your habits.

Whatever you can think of is fine, you know you will not be the best for a long time, so don't worry about being "ugly" meaning not perfect. Remember, done is the new perfect!

Combination

You can become an expert in any of the previous mentioned topics in this chapter, writing books, video content, music creation or online seminars.

If you are branding yourself as a coach for example like me, then a combination of these things will work wonders for your branding, then you are not thinking about the revenue streams when you create a book for example, but instead you are concentrating on the exposure that the book will have on your brand. You will Google how to create a best seller on Amazon like I have done, I have two best sellers on Amazon, I have published 4 books this year and it is May now, but it's all for branding. Now I will shift my focus on to the next thing and not publish another book this year. Shifting my focus around and creating a total branding strategy by combining all of these methods.

I am a coach and I do all the things mentioned in this chapter, I realize I can make a whole lot of money in any one of the topics discussed in the chapter, but I choose not to do that, because that is not my passion to be an expert in any one field.

I am a serial entrepreneur who loves to teach you how you can create wealth with many different methods. I love learning new things and for me each of these methods is an add-on to my success but not the focus. Your growth is my focus.

I know anyone can create wealth using any of the four methods talked about. I also know you have to be consistent and you have to be willing to give it 12 months before you can see any residual income that makes any difference to you.

Summary

- Building a pipeline of creation is based on simple small steps you puzzle together.

- Create a pipeline for video content and start getting advertisement revenue from the creation, and then in the future, possible product placement revenue and finally revenue from creating videos for others or partnering up with other video content creators. Give people value and they will follow you.

- Create a pipeline for music creation and start getting royalties from the creation.

- Create a pipeline for writing books. Keep publishing at average one book per month and you will be noticed very soon, and before you know it you will have nice income streams from the books that will gradually grow over time.

- Creating a pipeline for online courses, with at least two platforms you can create free online courses and paid online courses, which work very well together to create residual income from teaching through online courses.

- If you don't want to be an expert, you can use all 4 methods to brand yourself as authority figure in whatever field it is you are focused on.

13. No More Bad Habits

No More Bad Habits

Why do most people fail to reach success, when there is so much information showing them how to be very successful? Find out how your habits influence the potential success or failure you achieve.

People living today are extremely lucky because 50 years ago the internet did not even exist, and cable TV was something you read about in sci-fi magazines. Now, thanks to the internet, you can find information on practically anything you want, immediately. Something which was only a strange dream just one decade ago.

Yet with all this information available to us, people still fail to become successful in life. Why?

After all, there is so much support information available showing us how to be successful, but most people still fail to reach success.

And why do people still undergo depressions, when there are so many media's telling and showing them how to live a fantastic happy healthy life? The point is, information is not the problem.

And no matter how much technology advances, people will continuously have the identical problems.

Why People Fail To Achieve Success?

If you ask somebody why they not once succeeded in what they were trying to do, they will almost certainly tell you it was someone else's fault, or to some degree a thing happened that was beyond their control.

Yet if you compare those people's life against someone else's life, you could most likely find many illustrations of people who suffered under far inferior conditions yet still became very success.

This is showing that the real reason people fail is not because of something outside of them, rather the reason lies within them.

When you continue to do the same thing over and over again we call this a habit. You are undoubtedly familiar with bad habits such as smoking, drinking, gambling but are you familiar with the habits of failure or the habits of success?

Creating Habits of Success

Because success and failure are in the end achieved through the actions you take, habits therefore play a wonderful role in defining whether people will achieve success or failure in life. For example. If you read every day, that is a habit. This habit is likely to expand your knowledge of a topic, and vastly improve the chances you will master and be successful at it.

However, let's say that instead of reading every day, you prefer to sit down and watch a movie for a few hours. Do you think this will help you dominate any subject or become an expert in any field? For sure, the answer will be NO.

So if you want to achieve success or failure of the actions you repeat every day, then it is very simple to recognize why some people succeed, and others whine on their failure.

People who are successful constantly working on things and showing action to increase their chances of even more success. Unsuccessful people don't do any of this other than complain to as many people as possible.

This does not mean successful people will never fail, they do. But what they never do is giving up, because they have established fantastic habits of success.

Change Your Habits!

Think about what do you do on a daily basis, and ask yourself if those things help you achieve what you want in life? What are your daily good and daily bad habits? Be honest to yourself and firstly identify them.

Then make a selection of with habits move you forward towards success and bad habits pulling you back.

If the answer is no, then you must change those habits, because by doing the same thing over and over again you will only get the same results over and over again.

Start focusing in your good habits and start doing them daily. Eliminate the bad ones and after only 28 days this will become one more habit and you are on your way to great success.

14. Tying It All Together

Tying it all together

Now the time has come for you to take this gigantic leap forward and start your journey to the life you desire and deserve. What do you want?

We have covered vast distances of information for you to digest. Did you get the epiphany you needed to start today? Did you pick up something in the book that opened your eyes and you now believe it's possible for you to succeed? I know there is something in this book that has fueled that flame inside of you, that spark that has been waiting for fuel to be poured onto, to fuel that burning desire you need to succeed. Let me recap the process as well as I can to sum up the process of success.

Know what you want, or know what you don't want and turn that into a want. Once you have an idea of what you truly want to manifest into your reality, start to write down your future vision. Write your future based on your description of what you feel once this or that is done, once you have completed a task into your future. How does it feel, now that's it's already done?

Describe it like it's the now, but it's in the future, write your future as it's already done. Yes, it feels great!

Feed your mind every single day with positivity and knowledge. The smart human learns from his mistakes but you, the wise, learns from others peoples mistakes. By learning from other entrepreneurs mistakes you shorten the gap between now and your success journey.

You want to surround yourself with people who help you grow. People who are smarter, more successful, funnier and whatever you desire to become more of. You cannot grow in an environment where you are the smartest, richest, most successful person in the room.

Watch people who are doing what you strive to become, what you want to succeed at. Get a coach or mentor to train you. Get someone that you can ask for advice and get confirmation on your ideas and products and on your plans implementing anything in regards to your growth.

Brand yourself and brand your products.

Be visible online and create something that people can remember, something that will stick to their mind. Keep showing up online and outsource anything that you can, in regards to the online presence. There is no such thing as too much social media posting if you desire great growth and branding. To put it in perspective, there are some brands that post on social media every few seconds every day of the year.

Celebrate your little wins. Watch out for your haters, they are your signs of growth. The more people start to criticize you and hate on your growth the further you are on your journey to success. If you have already decided to avoid too much success because you can't handle anyone being mad at you or hating on you, then you have lost already. With even the smallest gains in your success story, there will be a person who does not like it somewhere.

There will be a person who will contact you and tell you that you should lay back, relax or quit. This person will probably be closer to you that you can imagine. A close friend or family member are likely to be one of your first critics.

Don't take it personally, instead celebrate it, not to their face of course, you don't want to throw gasoline on their hate fire.

Celebrate it in your own way and you don't need to tell anyone why you are celebrating your first hater or naysayer. Just do it, you are one step closer, it's a win for you.

What is your WHY? You have to have a reason that's bigger than you, to be able to endure long enough to reach the state of success. The state of success is the whole journey not just the destination. When you have a big enough reason to carry on, nothing can stop you, but you can be sure that something will come up or someone will try to convince you to stop on your way. Your WHY will keep you from even considering to quit.

Why are you doing this? If you have a great reason why, there is no objection strong enough to make you stop. If you encounter health issues with family or even death, attend your family, family should always come first, but you will get back to your journey once you have attended whatever is needed to attend to. Your WHY is strong!

Think about how many people don't go the distance because they cannot put themselves in the first place. The live their lives for someone else or live their lives like they think someone else wants them to do.

It is better to be hated for being you, than being loved for being something else. Your fulfillment in life will not come with living a life you think others want for you. Follow your heart and listen to your gut.

Get rid of your bad habits. Get rid of the habits that are holding you back. What habit can you start on today and which healthy habit or obsession can you use to replace that bad habit with?

You can obsess about something positive and replace the bad habit, starting as soon as you put this book down, or better yet just start right now. It is all a matter of deciding to, then seeking help if you need it and implementing it. Do not go cold turkey and hold your breath and hope the desire for that bad habit will disappear. Use that fuel, that energy, into the new obsession you are going to replace that habit with, right now.

Start implement what it is that you want to start doing. Use the chapter "The Pipeline" if you need step by step instructions of how to create cash flow by creating books, music, videos or online courses.

Create residual income for your journey. Totally depending upon you, what you want, but if you can start to create residual income in the field you want to live in and breathe or so to speak then it's important to start implementing it in your field of interest right of the bat.

Do not get caught in the idea of creating something just because it seems easy to do it and then when you make enough money doing that, then you will go into the field or industry you love. Many entrepreneurs have tried it that way, it does not work, you need that fire driving you on each day. You need to have that passion burning inside of you, fueling you into greatness. Start creating something you love to do or start talk about the things you love right now.

Your team is essential to your success, you will not make it on your own. At least it will take you much, much longer on your own. You need to leverage yourself by creating a team around yourself and your ideas. You will need talent around you, but it does not have to cost a lot like you can see in the chapter "The Pipeline". Outsourcing is a wonderful thing. Multiply yourself and get great things done in less time. You are ready! We can't wait to hear your success story soon!

Other Books by the Authors

Alexander Evengroen

http://AlexanderEvengroen.com

How to Become a Great Manager

You are what you Think

How to Become Successful

Huni Hunfjord

http://HuniHunfjord.com

Læringinn

The Mentorian

Top 1% Parents Raise Top 1% Children

Sleeping Habits and Routines

Now that you have all the secrets you have no more excuses on your way to greatness and awesomeness.

Put your shoulders under your dreams and start moving forward. This is the way you are heading.

No more looking back, you are not going that way. The horizon is your guide-line to change your lives, become the next millionaire or even billionaire. The sky is the limit.

The end of this amazing book is the start of an amazing new beginning for you.......

One Last Thing...

If you enjoyed this amazing book or found it useful we would be very grateful if you would post a short review on Amazon. Your support really does make a difference and we read all the reviews personally so we can get your feedback and make this book even better.

If you'd like to leave a review all you need to do is to go and review this book on Amazon here;

http://amazon.com/author/alexevengroen

http://amazon.com/author/hunihunfjord

If you have purchased a printed copy of the book, send your review directly to:

testimonial@OurRoadwithoutBoundaries.com as we would love to include your review on our website.

http://OurRoadwithoutBoundaries.com/

Thanks again for your support, keep being awesome!

Alexander Evengroen & Huni Hunfjord.

OUR ROAD
WITHOUT
BOUNDARIES
Revealing the Codes

www.ingramcontent.com/pod-product-compliance
Lightning Source LLC
Chambersburg PA
CBHW072259210326
41519CB00057B/1962